FLOYD CLYMER'S MOTORCYCLIST'S LIBRARY

The Book of the
CYCLEMOTOR

CLIP-ON MOTORS AND LIGHTWEIGHT
AUTOCYCLES: CHOOSING, RUNNING,
AND SERVICING THEM

BY

FERRERS LEIGH

First Edition 1954

ANNOUNCEMENT

By special arrangement with the original publishers of this book, Sir Isaac Pitman & Son, Ltd., of London, England, we have secured the exclusive publishing rights for this book, as well as all others in THE MOTORCYCLIST'S LIBRARY.

Included in THE MOTORCYCLIST'S LIBRARY are complete instruction manuals covering the care and operation of respective motorcycles and engines; valuable data on speed tuning, and thrilling accounts of motorcycle race events. See listing of available titles elsewhere in this edition.

We consider it a privilege to be able to offer so many fine titles to our customers.

FLOYD CLYMER
Publisher of Books Pertaining to Automobiles and Motorcycles

2125 W. PICO ST.   LOS ANGELES 6, CALIF.

INTRODUCTION

Welcome to the world of digital publishing ~ the book you now hold in your hand, while unchanged from the original edition, was printed using the latest state of the art digital technology. The advent of print-on-demand has forever changed the publishing process, never has information been so accessible and it is our hope that this book serves your informational needs for years to come. If this is your first exposure to digital publishing, we hope that you are pleased with the results. Many more titles of interest to the classic automobile and motorcycle enthusiast, collector and restorer are available via our website at www.VelocePress.com. We hope that you find this title as interesting as we do.

NOTE FROM THE PUBLISHER

The information presented is true and complete to the best of our knowledge. All recommendations are made without any guarantees on the part of the author or the publisher, who also disclaim all liability incurred with the use of this information.

TRADEMARKS

We recognize that some words, model names and designations, for example, mentioned herein are the property of the trademark holder. We use them for identification purposes only. This is not an official publication.

INFORMATION ON THE USE OF THIS PUBLICATION

This manual is an invaluable resource for the classic motorcycle enthusiast and a "must have" for owners interested in performing their own maintenance. However, in today's information age we are constantly subject to changes in common practice, new technology, availability of improved materials and increased awareness of chemical toxicity. As such, it is advised that the user consult with an experienced professional prior to undertaking any procedure described herein. While every care has been taken to ensure correctness of information, it is obviously not possible to guarantee complete freedom from errors or omissions or to accept liability arising from such errors or omissions. Therefore, any individual that uses the information contained within, or elects to perform or participate in do-it-yourself repairs or modifications acknowledges that there is a risk factor involved and that the publisher or its associates cannot be held responsible for personal injury or property damage resulting from the use of the information or the outcome of such procedures.

WARNING!

One final word of advice, this publication is intended to be used as a reference guide, and when in doubt the reader should consult with a qualified technician.

PREFACE

THOUSANDS of people of all ages have discovered in the last few years that the cyclemotor, the simple "clip-on" attachment which converts an ordinary pedal cycle into a power-assisted vehicle, solves their personal transport problems. THE BOOK OF THE CYCLEMOTOR has been written for the benefit of such people, as well as for those on the brink of discovery who have yet to make up their minds.

A representative selection of seventeen makes are described and illustrated from a practical point of view in these pages. The word "practical" is emphasized, since only details of direct service to those wishing to buy and use a cyclemotor are given. The compass of this book has not permitted explanations of how the two- and four-stroke engines work. Similarly references to carburettors and magnetos are limited to their make-up and maintenance. The student who wishes to learn the theory of engines and their accessories will find many excellent specialist books on the market.

The autocycle as such is not described in this book. Autocycles are heavier machines, generally with engines of 98 c.c., primarily designed to be ridden under power and not normally pedalled. The cyclemotor owner can, and frequently does, use his pedals as much as his engine, in the interests of exercise and economy. However, at least three borderline cases, which strictly come under the autocycle definition because they are sold only as complete machines, are included in the pages that follow. These three makes have engines of under 50 c.c. and they can be pedalled easily. And in two or three other cases makers of "clip-ons" can supply a complete bicycle designed around their units. These too can be pedalled and are true cyclemotor machines.

In general the cyclemotor is a simple little two-stroke engine, running on a mixture of oil and petrol ("petroil"), and attachable to any sound, well-shod bicycle in half an hour or less. The price range, complete, is from about £16–£40. Many of the more expensive types generate their own direct lighting and will even work a light electric horn (many people are unaware that motorized cycles may not be legally fitted with a bell to give warning of approach). When the cyclemotor is sold as a separate unit it qualifies as an accessory and escapes purchase tax. If the complete motorized cycle is sold purchase tax must be paid. Thus the prices of the ABJ, Mobylette, and VeloSoleX, within the range

PREFACE

of £42–£70, are considerably increased by tax. One maker solves this problem in a particularly ingenious way by supplying the cycle, if one is required, minus the back wheel. This wheel containing a built-in motor can then be purchased separately.

Most cyclemotors are single-speed machines with a drive ratio of about fifteen to one giving a road speed of fifteen to twenty miles per hour. One radically different production, the Italian Ducati "Cucciolo" (Little Pup), is a four-stroke of 48 c.c. with pull-rod overhead valves, positive lubrication from a separate oil tank, and a two-speed pre-selector gear. It drives through the pedalling chain.

The Lohmann, a German production, is another machine of specialized type which merits individual mention. Shown for the first time at Earl's Court in 1952, it is at the moment the smallest cyclemotor (only 18 c.c.) and the only example of compression ignition, having neither magneto nor carburettor. It is, however, still a single-speed unit of the two-stroke type running upon "petroil" fuel.

Methods of driving the cycle vary considerably. Five makes described in this book are mounted over the front forks of the cycle and propel the front tyre through a carborundum or patterned steel roller. Six more use a roller drive upon the back tyre, three from a position below the bottom bracket and three from behind the saddle in the place where a rear carrier is normally fitted.

Two that fit to the bottom bracket use a final drive by chain, one employing the pedalling chain and the other an additional chain and pinion at the near side of the rear wheel (as autocycles do). Three designs are built into or round the rear hub, and two of these transmit the final drive by chain to an extra sprocket on or within the rear wheel. The third uses gears.

Belts are favoured by two makers, one as a countershaft to a final chain drive. The other, a rear-carrier cyclemotor, connects a small pulley on the crankshaft to a large one on the rear spokes by an endless belt such as was used by many early motor cycles.

Six makers, whose designs otherwise vary widely, share in common the provision of a positive clutch. In five cases this is brought to a handlebar control exactly as in a larger motor-cycle, though one maker simplifies his clutch control by ingeniously combining it with the throttle twist-grip. In the remaining model the operation of the clutch is entirely automatic.

Without further elaboration of details it will be clear that the prospective buyer has a wide choice between the two extremes, represented by a simple workmanlike attachment, devoid of frills. at under twenty pounds, and an elaborate and handsome

PREFACE

affair of the autocycle type costing nearly seventy pounds. Much depends upon whether the buyer has or has not already a thoroughly sound pedal cycle with good tyres, a point emphasized in a short later chapter on road safety and the cyclemotor.

All the auxiliary motors on the market are sound and fit for even long-distance touring, as many owners have proved. People have ridden all over Europe on them, and they present no difficulty to anyone who can ride a pedal cycle. The rider, in this country at least, must be 16 or over.

For normal running, a few miles a day shopping, making calls, journeying to work and back, the buyer could pick a make with a pin. Any of them will give 200 and more trouble-free miles per gallon. Even with premium fuels at their present prices, and with compulsory tax and insurance, the cyclemotor-powered machine represents the cheapest possible form of personal transport; cheaper, as one maker points out, than walking! A push-cycle would perhaps be cheaper in basic cost alone, but the little extra speed of the powered machine enables distances to be covered which would be impossible to the unaided cyclist.

A rider wishing to cover hundreds of miles weekly, with or without steep hills, would do well to study at first machines with more than one gear, or with a choice of gear ratios. Even so, a little light pedalling will take the smallest cyclemotor up all but the steepest of single-figure gradients.

There is no need, either, to be unduly influenced by the position in which a maker recommends his machine to be fitted. Although the weight is only a few pounds, each maker claims that his particular model is designed to fit in the best and safest position. The buyer is puzzled because according to one this is over the front wheel, and to another, beneath the bottom bracket. Much more important is the rider's own position, and the safety aspect of this is brought out later on.

A final word to you, the reader, if you are looking at this book and hesitating whether to buy a "clip-on" or not. There is fun in this cyclemotor business. To the normal healthy person who has never had horse-power at command before, what exhilaration there is on a fine day to zip along with the little motor humming as it drives you! What pleasure to breathe the country air, to get to places at infinitesimal cost, to know that you can never get stuck because, if you misjudge your fuel, you can always pedal. What a thrill, for instance, to take the cycle to France on holiday, where you are welcomed as a friend because here half a nation rides, as you do, on the *vélomoteur*!

People are doing this every year now, here and abroad, people who thought they would always have to struggle on to expensive and uncomfortable buses and trains. They make their own

PREFACE

time-tables. They pack a couple of panniers on the back of the machine and push their horizon away from them. Why not you?

Do you realize that with any of the machines described in the pages that follow you could leave the south coast one morning and be riding along the Riviera five days later?—800-odd miles at a cost of twenty-five shillings for fuel. Five days on the road, five days there, five days coming back. . . .

Putting ideas in your head? I hope so!

F. L.

CONTENTS

CHAP.		PAGE
	Preface	
I.	LICENSING AND LAW	1
II.	ROAD SAFETY AND THE CYCLEMOTOR	6
III.	LOOKING AFTER YOUR CYCLEMOTOR	9
IV.	AMAL CYCLEMOTOR CARBURETTORS	16
V.	THE "BANTAMAG" MAGNETO	24
VI.	THE AUTO-MINOR (ABJ)	28
VII.	THE BERINI	32
VIII.	THE B.S.A. "WINGED WHEEL"	37
IX.	THE CYCLAID	41
X.	THE CYCLEMASTER	45
XI.	THE DUCATI "CUCCIOLO"	50
XII.	THE ITOM	56
XIII.	THE LOHMANN	58
XIV.	THE MINI-MOTOR	62
XV.	THE MOBYLETTE	69
XVI.	THE MOCYC	72
XVII.	THE MOSQUITO	75
XVIII.	THE POWER PAK	80
XIX.	THE TEAGLE	85
XX.	THE VAP 4	89
XXI.	THE VELOSOLEX	95
XXII.	THE VINCENT "FIREFLY"	102
	Index	107

CYCLEMOTORS AT A GLANCE (Prices subject to variation)

Makers' Name and Capacity (c.c.)	Engine Wt. (lb.)	Mounting and Drive	"Petrol" Mixture	Lighting Coils	Price (fitting extra)
ABJ Auto-Minor (49)	*	FF—R	1-20	Yes	£41 3s. 9d.–£42 13s. 2d.*
Berini (32)	15½	FF—R	1-25	No	£24
B.S.A. "Winged Wheel" (35)	27	RW—C—Cl	1-25	Yes	£25 with wheel and tyre
Cyclaid (31)	15	RC—Belt	1-30	No	£24
Cyclemaster (32—earlier 25·7)	26	RW—Ch—Cl	1-25	Yes	£27 10s. (replacement wheel)
Ducati "Cucciolo" (48)	17½	BB—Ch—Cl (2 speed)	Four-stroke	Yes	£40 (with cycle, £62 10s. 9d.)
Itom "Tourist" (48)	19	BB—R	1-16	Yes	£28 10s.
Lohmann (18)	11	BB—R	1-16 (compression-ign.)	No	£25 4s.
Mini-Motor (49·9)	26	RC—R	1-20	No	£18 10s.
Mobylette (49·9)	*	BB—Belt & Ch—Cl (automatic)	1-12	Yes	£49 16s.–£54 12s.
Mocyc (49)	20	FF—R	1-16	No	£16 16s.
Mosquito (38)	15	BB—R	1-16	No	£27 10s.
Power Pak (49)	22 & 25	RC—R & Cl (sync.)	1-16	No	£19 19s.–£27 6s. inc. tyre (special)
Teagle (49)	—	RC—R	1-20	No	£17
VAP-4 (48)	20	RW—Ch—Cl	1-12	No	£33
VeloSoleX (45)	*	FF—R	1-16	Yes	£38 8s.*
Vincent "Firefly" (48)	23¼	BB—G—R	1-25	Yes	£25

Abbreviations: FF—front forks. R—roller. RW—rear wheel. RC—rear carrier.
BB—bottom bracket. Cl—clutch is fitted. G—gear. Ch—chain.
* Sold as complete autocycle.

CHAPTER I

LICENSING AND LAW

THERE are certain formalities with which you must comply before you can ride your new cyclemotor-equipped machine upon the road. Your dealer will attend to the formalities for you if you have no wish to be bothered with them, but it is essential that you should at least know about them.

Registration. First, the machine must be registered with the local licensing authority. Your dealer will arrange this for you, and will see that the correct form (R.F.1/2) is filled up and signed by you. This is forwarded with a "Certificate of Insurance," and the appropriate sum, 17s. 6d. annually, 4s. 10d. quarterly, and pro rata, to the motor licensing department of the County Council or County Borough Council in whose area you reside.

In return the machine receives official recognition, taking the form of a log book—really a folded card—in which particulars of the machine and of all licences issued are entered. The log book is stamped with certain letters and figures: the registration symbols which have to be displayed fore and aft on your cycle and probably taking the form of three capital letters followed by three figures. In some districts the figures now precede the letters, and there may be four figures followed by one letter.

The registration symbols have to be displayed in two sizes. The front plate can be small and clipped to the handlebars if you favour a forward-reading plate. Alternatively it must be shown at each *side* of the front wheel of your machine, *which the law now regards as a motor-cycle*. There can be a double-sided plate curved to fit the front mudguard as you will have seen on larger motor cycles. Alternatively the numbers and letters can be painted or otherwise shown upon a convenient flat surface such as the fuel tank on one side and the magneto casing on the other, as in the VeloSoleX machine.

You can have the registration marks applied by transfer, quite durable if they are varnished (painted on is not so durable), or you can spend a bit more and have aluminium plates with polished "silver" figures; naturally the most durable.

At the back the plate and registration marks have to be larger. Whereas the front plate or plates show the whole thing in one line, XYZ 123, the back plate has them in two rows: $\frac{XYZ}{123}$. Other variants are $\frac{123}{ABC}$, or $\frac{1234}{A}$ (the figures *must* be in one line as here). The back plate must be illuminated at night with a white light in addition to the red light you display.

The dimensions of the letters and figures and the distance between them are precisely laid down by law. If you buy transfers from a dealer these will be the right size. It is only sensible to see that your registration marks are the legal ones. Do not try and paint them yourself; do not use the white figures sold in the multiple stores for screwing to the front gate!

Because people do these things with apparent impunity proves nothing. The saving is negligible—the result might, conceivably, be a disqualified driving licence.

Another item that has to be put on the machine is the licence disc. It can go anywhere, roughly speaking, between the handlebars and the front spindle as long as it faces to the near or pavement side. The licence is supposed to be contained in a weatherproof holder with a *glass* front—not plastic. Here again, thousands flout the law and know nothing about this.

Leave it to your dealer. It is his job to see that these many little regulations are complied with. And one other matter before you take the road—remove that bell from your handlebars. Once again, hundreds get away with it. But motor-cycles, such as yours now is in the eyes of the law, are not allowed to carry bells to give warning of approach. No, you must have a "pip-pip" bulb, or a light electric horn, if your coils will feed it, or a grater—the kind of mechanical horn that the French call a *klaxon* and that sounds like someone clearing his throat!

Insurance. One cannot take all these things quite in their logical order, but at least you know what has to happen about the bicycle. Now we must retrace our steps and have an understanding of the insurance regulations.

You must be covered against third-party risks to be even *in charge* of a motor vehicle—which could mean standing at the roadside without the engine running. How much does insurance cost? Very approximately the minimum legal insurance—which gives no cover for damage to the cycle—is about ten shillings a year. For something like thirty shillings you can extend the policy to cover the cycle against damage or loss.

Please go into this very carefully with the dealer and your own insurance company, or both, before making a final decision. There are many factors, including whether you live in town or country, which affect the amount of premium you pay.

There is the type of cover, for instance, known as "third party, fire, and theft," which adds to the essential legal cover loss by fire or stealing, but not damage. Many careful people find this enough.

If you specify on your proposal form that only *you* will ever ride the machine, you may be able to get a reduction in premium on this account. If it is solely for your personal use there is no point in paying extra for non-existent alternative riders. But you must at all times remember that you have made this arrangement with your insurers, and not unthinkingly lend it to a workmate, or to Uncle Tom to post the letters one day.

Another tip to keep costs down is to undertake to pay the first £5, or what you will, of any claim. This is a safe form of economy very popular with underwriters to whom niggling little claims are an infernal nuisance. Anyway it is hoped that enough has been written here to make you look carefully into the insurance policy before signing the proposal form and posting it off with the premium.

When you have done this, you will receive a bulky envelope containing a large fold-up document, which is the policy. Most people seem to put this away without looking at it. Don't—study it with care. Snags can still crop up—for instance, it is better to discover now, rather than on the day before you are due to start on your holiday abroad, that you are not covered for sea transit or for continental travel.

There will also be a rather intimidating-looking claims form, which with luck you will never need to use. But examine it all the same; more of this a little later when we discuss the reporting of accidents.

The other document in the envelope is the indispensable "Certificate of Insurance"—a small sheet, notepaper size, headed with the words just quoted. (You may get a provisional cover note, if the insurance is being effected in a hurry, which keeps you going for fifteen days, or perhaps a month, and which serves the same purpose as the certificate.)

The certificate must be sent to the taxation authorities with the log book, the signed application form, and the remittance, each time you apply for a Road Fund licence. Thousands of people still send their *policies* with their applications, which are no good at all to the motor-taxation clerks. Each time a licence is issued the certificate is date-stamped the same as the log book.

The log book will not have been issued when you make a first application, so send the money (cheque or postal order), the form (R.F.1/2), and the essential "Certificate of Insurance." For subsequent applications use form R.F.1 A obtainable from all but sub-post-offices and, of course, from local taxation offices.

Tuck the policy away in your desk after you have studied it, but keep the certificate in a safe but accessible place. You may be asked for it at any time by a police officer. The police often have routine check-ups and it certainly does not follow that because you have not been involved in an accident you will never be asked for your certificate.

If and when you are asked for the certificate, you are not obliged to produce it on the spot, but if you cannot you will be requested to show it at any police station of your own choosing within 48 hours. As this can lead to inconvenience, if say you are miles away on holiday and have left it at home, the author recommends his own practice of folding the certificate up small and retaining it in the driving licence with a rubber band. And that now brings us to the question of the driving licence itself.

Provisional Licences. Unless you already have such a licence—and if so, make sure that it does cover riding a motor cycle, as it will if it is for "All Groups"—you must add to your application for a Road Fund Licence a request also for a Provisional Driving Licence, costing 5s., made on form D.L.1. You can add this amount to the sum you are sending for the Road Fund Licence.

The Provisional Licence is valid for three months, and must be renewed at the end of this time. Until you qualify for a full licence you have to display regulation "L" plates on your machine, one fore and one aft. These, as you will doubtless have noticed, are square white plates with a red "L" upon them. You can get a regulation pair of plates on card very cheaply, so do resist the temptation to scrawl an "L" on a postcard and try to get away with it.

The Driving Test. You can apply to take the driving test on form D.L.26 (obtainable from the post office together with the address of the nearest Clerk of the Traffic Area, to whom a fee of 10s. is payable) six weeks from the day you receive the Provisional Licence, and no sooner. You have, therefore, plenty of time to get used to road work, and if the worst comes to the worst you can go on taking it at six-weekly intervals and renewing your Provisional Licence as needed.

With your Provisional Licence you will receive a copy of *The Highway Code*, a simple, straightforward, illustrated statement of the road user's responsibilities and rights. It should, in effect, be learned by heart before you go for the test; particularly, the hand signals should be thoroughly studied and absorbed.

The Highway Code has not the force of law. But most accidents are caused by failure to observe it, and especially its provisions about turning. In these, unfortunately, many cyclists are offenders. Resolve, at least for your own safety, not to be numbered among them.

LICENSING AND LAW

The test is given by a Ministry of Transport examiner. If, before taking to a cyclemotor, you already have considerable experience as a pedal cyclist, it will present no difficulties to you. The thing to remember is not to rush at it. You cannot take it for six weeks, and after that you have a further six weeks in which to practise before your first provisional licence is due for renewal; therefore, don't hurry. As soon as you have passed the test you can remove the "L" plates and take out an annual licence (Group G) costing a further 5s.

At the moment the law, by which the rider of a motorized cycle, after passing the test, can drive a high-powered motor cycle or a three-wheeler (with no reverse gear), is under examination. This state of affairs is held by many to be wrong, but if a new class of road user—to which you would belong—is brought into being, this will not affect you at all.

It has taken quite a time and many words to detail the points which the law requires you to observe in this country. As with many seemingly complicated things, it takes longer to tell than to do. Another thing, it all sounds rather expensive. In fact it is not, or there would not be so many cyclemotorists on the road.

Licences, number plates, "L" plates, licence holder, insurances; the whole lot should come to less than five pounds a year, even in these expensive days. That is about two shillings a week.

Accidents. A few final words about a disagreeable subject before we leave the law: what to do in an accident. The golden rule is—if you do have an accident, keep your head and control your emotions.

Accidents must be reported to the police (the nearest policeman or a police station) if they involve injury to other people, or to animals (cats, for some odd reason, excepted) or to other people's property, vehicles, and so on. If you fall off and bend your own machine or yourself only, the police are not legally concerned.

Your insurance company will also expect a detailed report from you, on one of their claim forms, upon any accident likely to result in a claim upon them. Admit no liability, and get witnesses if you possibly can. If it is a bad write-off, either for you or for the other fellow, let the policeman write his report before you start pulling the wreckage about—except, of course, what you may have to do to help an injured person.

This little book cannot enter into further details. The next chapter, however, is entitled "Road Safety." It will tell you how to avoid mishaps and keep yourself and the insurance company happy and to make sure of that "no claim bonus" at the end of every year. It is a bold statement; "That every accident is avoidable," but it is true, and we shall try to show you how.

CHAPTER II

ROAD SAFETY AND THE CYCLEMOTOR

ROAD casualty figures show, unfortunately, a great many accidents to vehicles described as "motor cycles." Dr. Glanville of the Department of Scientific and Industrial Research, in an exhaustive inquiry into all aspects of road safety, has revealed that a high proportion of these accidents are concerned with cycles fitted with auxiliary motors. He has declared that defects in brakes and lighting are main causes.

Checking Over Your Cycle. It is unwise to fit any cyclemotor to any bicycle without first giving the machine a most careful check-over. The engine does impose extra strains and stresses, and the appreciable increase in average speed will soon find out weak spots in the cycle parts. Some cycles are, frankly, unsuitable for motorization.

Three of the cyclemotors described in this book are sold only as components of complete motorized bicycles which are, in fact, lightweight autocycles. In at least three other cases makers of cyclemotors, while supplying them as separate fittings, themselves sell or recommend a cycle designed to suit their own auxiliary engines.

If, therefore, you contemplate fitting a motor to your present cycle, the cycle should be checked over and reconditioned. A great many pedal cycles in daily use have imperfect brakes. The cyclemotor, raising the rider's average speed, makes it much more difficult to stop quickly. Some cyclemotors incorporate a back-pedalling brake which gives the rider an extra margin of safety.

Dr. Glanville's criticism of lighting applies with particular force to the bad rear lights seen—or not seen—on many machines. Here again the cyclemotor may make an improvement if lighting coils are incorporated in the magneto. If not, the rider should fit the best possible front and rear lighting to his machine.

In checking over a machine to see if it is suitable for motorization, bad condition and looseness will frequently be found in the steering-head. The bearings settle down and few people ever seem to think of taking up the play. Put your fingers underneath the handle-grips and lift—just short of the point at which the front tyre leaves the ground. If you can detect slack at the top steering-head bearing, it is high time something was done about it.

Next, both wheels should be scrupulously examined. Spin them to make sure that the rims are true. Lightly flick the spokes and listen for those that buzz or for one that is loose. Satisfy yourself that the hub bearings run free, without crackles or tight patches betraying worn cones or broken balls. You cannot expect to maintain 15–20 m.p.h. on the roads without true, free-spinning wheels.

Tyres should have plenty of tread, especially where the motor is driven by roller. If the inner tubes are not sound and reasonably new, then they will not be able to sustain the hard tyre pressures which the makers of your cyclemotor recommend. They should be really hard, blown up to the point at which, to your finger and thumb, the resilience seems to have disappeared.

See that all fittings on the machine are firmly secured. That flapping front mudguard could be shaken loose and throw you from the machine. That stripped saddle-bolt could make you lose your balance.

Having run the rule over the machine, spend a few minutes on your riding position. Sitting on the saddle, you should be able to put the balls of both feet—not just one—on the ground. This makes a vast difference to your safety and comfort in traffic. If the saddle height is correct you should be able to put your toes underneath the pedals at their lowest points. This will automatically mean that you can touch the ground comfortably at either side.

There is no fixed rule about handlebar angles or the angle of the rider's body. But having fixed the saddle for height, remember that it will also adjust fore and aft. The handlebars too have an adjustment for height. A comfortable rider is a safe rider.

Starting. Starting the cyclemotor, where this is of the kind driving by a roller on the tyre, has an important safety aspect. Most makers urge that the rider should lower the roller to the tyre and pedal away with the decompressor open. Then the decompressor is closed, the throttle is opened, and the engine fires.

On some makes the rider can raise or lower the roller by a handlebar, or other control, while pedalling. In this case there is the temptation to pedal off with the roller up, and then let the stationary roller down on to the moving tyre. If this is done suddenly the wheel may lock, throwing the rider, or lumps of rubber may be torn out of the tyre.

One cyclemotor maker does, however, design his engine to be started by gently lowering the roller on to the tyre. *Gently* is the operative word. The two-stroke engine resists being spun from rest unless the compression is first released. Therefore, on a dry rough road the tyre might be able to spin the roller, but on a smooth wet road, or a frosty one, the resistance of the engine could more easily overcome the grip between tyre and road, and so cause a skid.

Whatever the method of starting, avoid the risk of skidding by smooth and gentle treatment of the controls. If a decompressor is fitted, always use it at the outset.

Speed. This is the primary cause of most accidents. Most people ride a pedal cycle at 10–15 m.p.h. *The purpose of a cyclemotor is not to enable the rider to go faster, but to eliminate the exertion.* Another ten miles an hour introduces all sorts of complications and is a strain on the machine as well as on the rider. It is much more difficult to stop from higher speeds, even with the decompressor fully open.

By fitting a cycle speedometer and observing your speed you will be able to go comfortably and economically up to a 20 m.p.h. maximum. If you want to go faster you should get a lightweight motor-cycle. The speedometer, which costs less than two pounds, will also record your mileage and make maintenance and upkeep much simpler.

And that brings us to the next question we shall try to answer. What does looking after a cyclemotor entail?

CHAPTER III

LOOKING AFTER YOUR CYCLEMOTOR

Just like every other kind of engine, your new cyclemotor unit has to be run-in. When it is new, its assembly is very stiff, and what you have to do is to treat it kindly so that it will settle down to a long and serviceable life. This is much easier to do if you have some kind of mileage recorder, which will also enable you to keep a check on your fuel consumption. Therefore, if your cycle has not already got some form of mileage recorder, it is useful, though not essential, to fit one.

If you do not want to spend much money, a good cyclometer on the front hub will record the miles you cover. A speedometer plus mileometer on the handlebars will also tell you how fast you are going, but it will cost a little more.

As a rough guide to the progress of your engine, the first 500 miles will see it reasonably well run in and settled down. After the second 500 miles it should be running at its best. The object of the present chapter is to acquaint you with the simple rules by which these objects can be achieved.

Running-in: the First 500 Miles. When the engine is brand new, use the pedals quite freely to help it. The cyclemotor has a pretty hard life, and should thrive on hard work. Most of the time it gets a fully-open throttle, and it will take this much better if, while new, the pedal is freely used. There is no need to pedal hard. When getting away from a standstill keep the cranks turning easily. Do this for the first 100 or so miles whenever you accelerate, and give the engine help on all up-grades, even slight ones. Later it will probably be quite unnecessary.

With the two-stroke particularly, the first few miles are highly important because the piston has a job to do on its up strokes as well as the down ones. Therefore, the better the eventual fit between piston and cylinder, the better it will work on the up strokes when it is pumping the next charge of mixture into the crankcase.

It is a very good idea to strain all the fuel through a chamois, or a very fine gauze filter, before pouring it into the tank. Mix the petrol and oil thoroughly beforehand in a clean can. It is not essential, but it *is* most helpful, to add about a teaspoonful of graphited running-in compound to each tank of fuel. This of course would be over and above the recommended petrol-oil ratio, which should otherwise be strictly followed.

If you try to hurry up the running-in process, especially in hot weather, a piston may seize. You can always recognize this before it happens by a loss of power and a hollow choked sound from the exhaust. The thing to do is to disconnect *at once* the drive to the road wheel and close the throttle. Always shut the throttle and if a seizure catches you unawares, open the decompressor, put on the brake, and dismount as quickly as possible.

A seizure need be neither serious nor damaging. Just let the engine cool for a minute or two and then try it again, to see if the piston has freed, with drive "on" and the decompressor open. It is always best, if you do get a seizure, to have a look at the piston as soon as possible. Your dealer will do it if you are not able yourself. Sometimes the piston "grows" permanently and a new one must be fitted. Almost always the cause is the same—you cannot hurry up the running-in process.

Running-in: at 500 Miles. Let it be assumed that you have reached your 500 miles without incident. At this mileage it is a good idea to unscrew the sparking plug and have a look at the points. If they are blackish-grey with the tips much lighter and clean-looking, put it back and carry on. The mixture is perhaps a little rich, but does not need alteration for the second 500 miles.

If the points are black and wet-looking, right up to the firing tips, shake the plug out with a few drops of petrol (neat), or benzole, brush the points clean with a few light strokes from a fine wire brush, and let the plug dry before replacing it. A plug in this condition indicates an over-rich mixture. Check first that the maker's recommendation as to petrol-oil mixture is being followed. If so, then lower the carburettor needle one notch (see Chapter IV)—or, ask the garage to do it.

The third possible state of the plug points is unlikely in a two-stroke, but not inconceivable. If they look burned, dry, and biscuit-coloured, the fuel is too weak. Check for too little oil in the fuel or for a carburettor needle set too low.

Running-in: at 1,000 miles. It is now time to spend a few minutes checking the little thimble filters in the fuel line for sediment. If any is present, a certain amount of mud will have seeped through to the carburettor bowl. A few minutes at these points once every 1,000 miles or so can save a lot of messy tinkering by the roadside. Of course if you do filter every drop of your fuel you will not get sediment.

The next important thing at 1,000 miles is to take off the exhaust pipe and silencer at the port. Make sure that they are clear, and meticulously remove all traces of carbon from the exhaust port itself. Pick it out with a pointed chip of hardwood—

use no steel or iron tools for this job, and especially not that old screwdriver or wood chisel!

If the silencer is of ferrous metal, iron, that is, either sheet or casting, you can soak it overnight in a caustic soda solution. Anhydrous caustic soda is sold in pound tins and one pound dissolved in a gallon of water—or similarly a quarter pound in two pints—makes an effective working strength. If it is heated it is still more efficient and will shift any carbon deposit overnight.

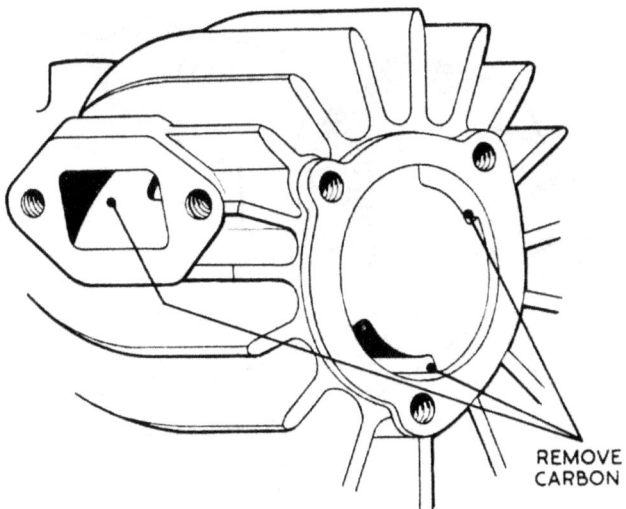

Fig. 1. Points to Note when Decarbonizing

But—some don'ts. *Don't use caustic soda with any aluminium or alloy parts;* it simply dissolves them. Remember, only iron or steel. It takes off everything, paint, carbon, jointing, right down to the bare metal. If you dunk your *iron* cylinder barrel in it to shift the carbon from the recesses of the transfer port, it will strip every trace of oil from the bore.

When making up the solution, add caustic soda a little at a time to the water—never the other way round. Considerable heat and energy is liberated. Don't get it on your hands or it will flay your skin. Handle the engine parts with tongs and if you get splashed wash it off at once under running water. But don't be frightened of the stuff. Just treat it with respect and keep it out of the way, tightly sealed up, when not wanted.

The Sparking Plug. If your 14 mm. sparking plug has two nuts it is detachable and is meant to be taken apart for cleaning. Put it upside down in a vice, holding the gland nut in the jaws.

Unscrew the outer shell with a plug spanner. Don't take the plug apart any other way save with the worm-drive tool some plug makers sell for the job. Other strippings will almost certainly spoil it. A plug is a precision instrument.

Soak the outer shell in caustic, or scrape it out carefully with an old penknife blade. Wipe off the centre electrode with a rag soaked in a little petrol. Polish the insulation and the inside of the shell. Reassemble, not forgetting the gland-nut washer. Set

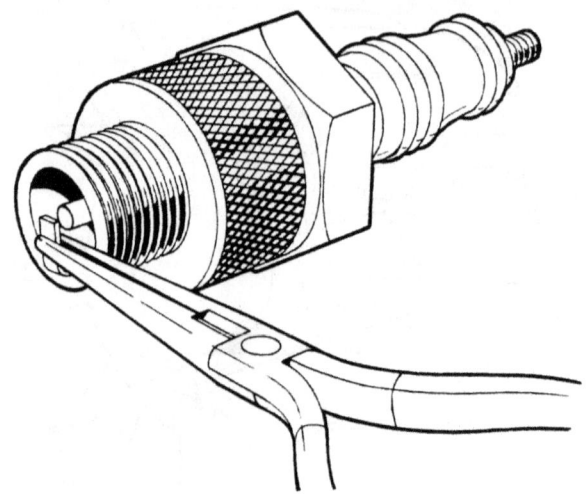

FIG. 2. REGAPPING A SPARKING PLUG

the gap to the thickness of your thumbnail by bending the outside —never the centre—electrode with fine-nosed pliers. If you tap with a hammer you will overdo it.

In replacing the plug in the cylinder head there is another copper-asbestos ring-washer to remember. You must put it back or you will never get a gas-tight joint. Keep a few spare washers by you—they are always getting lost. Do not over-tighten the plug in the head. Like turning a tap off, just compress the washer slightly.

Two-strokes seldom give trouble. When they do, it is the author's experience over many years that the cause should be sought, first of all, at one of three points: sparking plug, exhaust system, or magneto points—or a combination of all three.

Plugs are subject not only to oiling-up but to a mysterious malady—especially when overheated—known as "whiskering." A bridge grows from one electrode to the other and of course the plugs stops firing. What is this "bridge"? It seems to be metal,

LOOKING AFTER YOUR CYCLEMOTOR

some heat product drawn from the centre electrode. Many people say it is nickel. It can, of course, be removed by a flick of a penknife blade, but a plug that has once started to whisker is really of no further use save as an emergency spare.

One remedy for whiskering is to use a sports or even a racing plug, both designed to stand extra heat. On a Continental run in severe heat the author was advised by a garage to fit a plug with

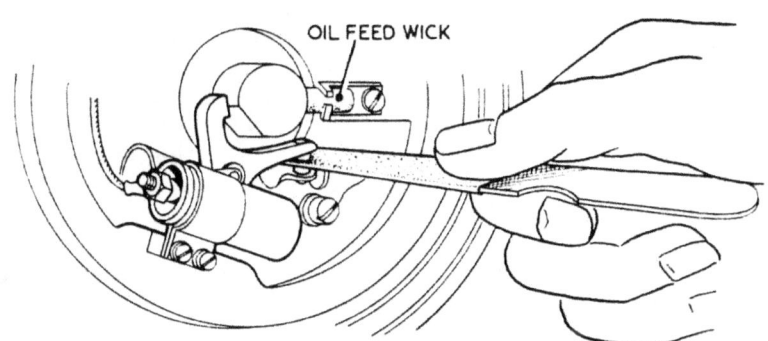

FIG. 3. CLEANING THE MAGNETO POINTS
This can be done with a stiff slip, such as a nail file, wrapped in a fold of fine grade emery cloth or paper.

a needle-centre electrode of platinum. It cost the equivalent of about fifteen shillings but there was no more plug trouble.

The Exhaust System. If the burnt gases cannot get out of the engine quickly, the engine cannot run properly. Carbon formation is more rapid round the exhaust port than anywhere else, and if the mixture is rich carbon will form twice as fast. A choked exhaust causes over-heating, loss of power, persistent four- and eight-stroking, and difficult starting.

The Magneto Points. This book includes a short illustrated chapter on the Wico-Pacy "Bantamag," standard equipment on most cyclemotors in Britain, and there is some general reference there to magneto-points adjustment. Here, however, we touch on the main considerations.

The points have a rough time. They snap together and reopen many times each second and they are subjected to thousands of volts' pressure. Small wonder that with this heat and battering they chip and burn.

They should be clean, should meet squarely, and should part to a gap of approximately 20 thousandths. The best way of cleaning them is to press them gently together with a thin slip, such as an old nail file, wrapped in a fold of very fine (00 grade) emery paper, gripped lightly between the flats of the points. Rub slowly to and fro, inspecting the points frequently and resetting the slip and emery each time.

Treat this as a precision operation and do not try to hurry it. Remember that without a lathe you cannot skim the points down truly flat or even slightly domed as some people say they should be.

Set the gap with equal care. Too small a gap gives very easy starting, but, misfiring and loss of power at touring speeds. Too wide a gap reverses these troubles. Despite the claim made by one cyclemotor manufacturer that the gap does not matter, it does. The limits are 0·018 to 0·025 in., generally speaking (one or two makers recommend a smaller gap), and the figure in your instruction book has, you may depend on it, been arrived at with painstaking research as the best for your engine.

Trouble Tracing. Although we hope you will never have starting trouble, a simple drill can be summed up by which either variety of trouble can be quickly remedied.

Firstly: when it won't start—

The engine is bound to start if (*a*) the proper "petroil" to air mixture is getting into it, (*b*) if the sparking plug is giving a spark to ignite this mixture, and (*c*) if the exhaust gases can afterwards get out of the engine. Therefore check:

That there is fuel in the tank (*a*) and that it can get out of the tank and into the carburettor. Resist, at this stage, the temptation to dismantle the carburettor, as this is about the last thing that ever goes wrong on a two-stroke.

After checking the fuel and still getting no start, tackle the sparking plug (*b*). Remove this and put your thumb over the hole while you spin the engine. At the same time get a friend to hold the insulated part of the plug lead so that the metal end is against the engine. You should feel a regular alternate suction and pressure on the ball of your thumb, and at the same time sparks should flash between the end of the plug lead and the engine.

If so, the plug is faulty. Always have a sound, preferably new, spare at hand. Screw this in, connect up, and ten-to-one your trouble is over.

If there is no spark from the plug lead, the magneto points are next in line of inquiry. Remove the cover plate and examine them closely with an electric torch. If they look dirty, they may have bridged. The use of a petrol-damped rag, or a long fine brush with a drop of petrol on the bristles, will remedy this. Make sure the points do open and close.

If (*c*) there is petrol present and a spark, but the engine fires

LOOKING AFTER YOUR CYCLEMOTOR

and stops again, the trouble must be in the exhaust—the spent gases cannot get out. Quick check: remove the exhaust system bodily at the port. If the engine then starts and runs, the exhaust is "bunged-up" and must be cleared with caustic soda or a gas flame.

If the plug you have just removed is wet with liquid fuel, you have overdone the choking and flooding, which makes the engine as unstartable as if there were no fuel present. Shut the throttle and, with the plug still out, spin the engine a dozen times or so, to ventilate it. You still need to put in a spare dry plug after this.

Excessive richening is a common cause of engine "sulks" in two-strokes, particularly where the cylinder is upside down or sideways so that the fuel cannot drain away from the plug. Always flood the carburettor very sparingly.

Second trouble: when the engine dies on the road. Remedy: fuel check as before. If it spat and missed first, fuel shortage is the most likely answer. But if you were running hard and there had been a gradual drying-up feeling with a "woolly" exhaust, a whiskered plug is almost certainly the cause.

The offending plug being extremely hot, you will be glad you brought a 14 mm. box spanner. Substitute the good new spare you carry which has been wrapped up against damage in the tool-kit. The whiskered plug should be scrapped.

On resuming, run more gently, or you may whisker the spare too. Whiskering indicates overheating and you may have closely escaped an engine seizure—another reason for taking it easy.

If you live in hilly country, don't use the decompressor to excess when running downhill. The air-swirl throws any wet mixture present over the plug points. Similarly don't make long descents using the engine as a brake. With the throttle closed no oil—it being in the petrol—reaches the engine parts, which are therefore unlubricated! Since you cannot open the throttle downhill, take the engine off drive altogether—but make sure your brakes are efficient.

CHAPTER IV

AMAL CYCLEMOTOR CARBURETTORS

Two types of Amal carburettor are produced specifically for cyclemotors up to 40 c.c. capacity, and these notes are taken from descriptive literature by courtesy of Amal Ltd. One or other of these carburettors is fitted to many of the cyclemotors described in this book. They are of the single lever control type and have almost the same external appearance.

The A type. The carburettors of this type are stamped with the numbers 259, 359; 261, 361; or 265, 223, and have a needle in the throttle and only one jet under the jet cap. Type 308 is essentially the same as an A type, but has a bottom feed. When the type number begins with a 3, the float chamber may be secured with two screws. This carburettor is designed to eliminate any difficulty arising out of the use of very small jets. Control is automatic, a lever on the handlebar operating the throttle which in turn controls the mixture according to engine speed.

Full-power mixture-control is by the main jet feeding the engine through a needle jet in which there is a tapering needle. The taper on this affects the mixture at lesser throttle openings, and the position of the taper in the needle jet enrichens or weakens the mixture at various throttle positions.

The needle is located in the throttle by a circular spring clip held down by the throttle spring. The needle is itself positioned by one of five grooves around which the clip engages.

For idling, the fuel supply is controlled by the parallel portion of the needle entering the bore of the needle jet, the difference in diameter constituting the jet orifice. Obstruction or gumming up, due to the petrol and oil system, can be instantly cleared by opening the throttle.

Petrol is fed into the top of the float chamber where a constant level is maintained. Petrol at this level flows upwards to the main jet through a slanting passage. Air-locks are liberated through a second, higher, passage, slanting upwards from the needle-assembly into the top of the float chamber.

Access to the jets is gained by unscrewing the jet plug at the base. The throttle and adjustable needle can be removed by unscrewing the top of the mixing chamber. A set screw in the side of the mixing chamber engages a vertical groove in the throttle barrel and so guides its movement. A second slot in the throttle enables the control cable to be quickly detached.

Frequently the carburettor intake is fitted with an air cleaner, and a strangler for closing off the air when starting from cold. The air intake or gauze must be kept free from obstruction. If of the oil-wetted wire-wool type this should be periodically removed,

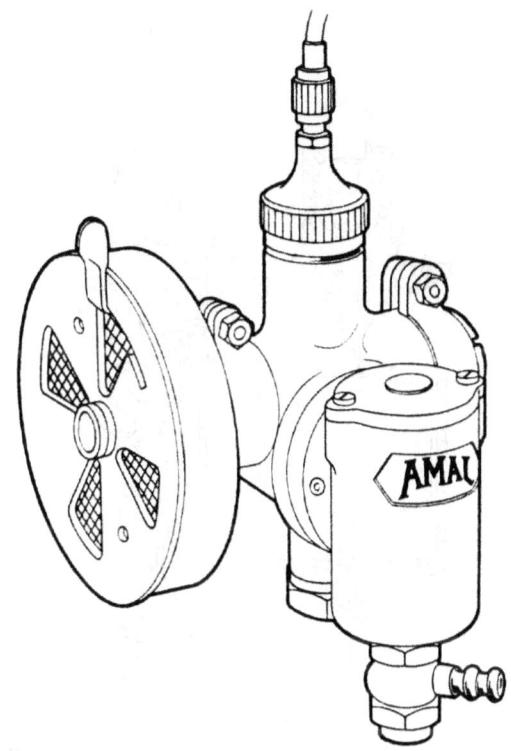

Fig. 4. The Small Amal Carburettor (Bottom Feed Type)

doused in commercial grade petrol and, when dry, re-oiled before being replaced. The air strangler or choke, if of the knife type, should remain firmly open or closed in either position. Should it become too loose and tend to creep, it should be bent slightly to stiffen its movement.

Flooding is perhaps the commonest carburettor trouble. Keep the float chamber free from impurities which are the main cause of flooding. If flooding persists the petrol-pipe connections must be removed from the lid and all passages cleaned. See that the float needle is not bent nor the float petrol-logged.

The needle seating may be at fault. Rub it lightly in by twisting the needle between the finger and thumb, but do not use grinding compound. A deep groove on the taper end of the needle indicates the probable need for a new needle (and float).

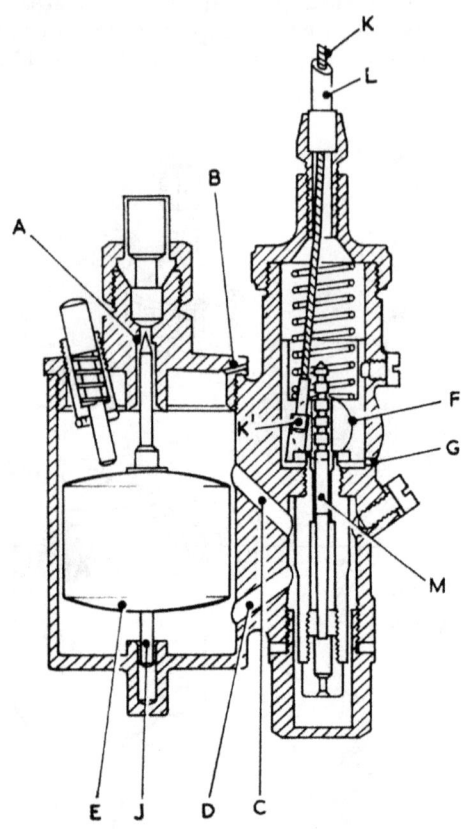

FIG. 5. THE SMALL AMAL CARBURETTOR (TOP FEED TYPE)

A. Needle seat.
B. Float chamber bleed.
C, D. Fuel feed passages.
E. Float.
F. Choke intake.
G. Slow running bleed.
J. Float bearing.
K, K^1. Control cable and nipple.
L. Cable casing.
M. Adjustable needle.

The tickler or flooder must work freely and spring back readily. The small air inlet B in the rim of the float-chamber lid often becomes obstructed unnoticed, and must be kept clear. Clean out impurities that may have accumulated in the needle guide at the bottom of the float chamber.

Incautious dismantling or reassembly can do considerable damage. Before replacing the float-chamber lid make sure that the blunt end of the float needle is in the guide hole at the bottom of the chamber. Then guide the lid over the taper end of the needle before screwing it down.

If the carburettor is removed from the induction pipe push it right home on the pipe before locking the ring clip, otherwise undetected air leaks can occur. The carburettor must be a good push-fit on the induction pipe and should be worked right home with a screwing motion after a little oil has been put on the pipe. Never fit a carburettor to a pipe on which it is slack, or force it on to a pipe on which it is obviously too tight.

If the throttle becomes slack after long use, the piston-effect is lost, and this will impair the slow running. Also, a throttle worn slack communicates its side movement to the needle and this wears the needle jet, making it too large in diameter. It should be replaced along with the throttle, or the mixture will become too rich and petrol consumption will go up. Sometimes a temporary remedy lies in lowering the needle, but a new needle jet is the better solution.

Faults and tuning can only be dealt with if the engine is otherwise in good order and the exhaust system is not choked with carbon. Check, first of all, the petrol supply, compression, and sparking plug. Then make sure there is no flooding and that the throttle and air strangler open and close completely, and that the air intake and gauze are clean.

The carburettor must also be clean internally, with jet and passages clear and main and needle jets screwed up firmly. There must be no air leak at the fitting of the carburettor to the engine (check both the mounting on the induction pipe and the point where the pipe is bolted to the cylinder).

Bad running can then be ascribed only to one of two things; weakness or richness of mixture. First, it must be established which condition is present, and second, at which throttle opening. Richness shows in black sooty exhaust smoke, petrol spraying from carburettor, four-stroking in a two-stroke, heavy petrol consumption, sooting of sparking plug, and lumpy running. Weakness produces spitting in the carburettor, erratic slow running, poor acceleration, better running at less than full throttle, overheating, and gives dry grey colour at sparking plug points.

Causes of richness are punctured float, bent float needle, flooder-button stuck down, needle raised too high, main jet too large or not screwed up, needle jet worn, or air filter choked. Weakness is caused by air-leaks, obstruction in petrol supply or jet partly choked, bent needle and/or impurities in needle guide beneath float chamber preventing float dropping, too small main jet, needle too low, air gauze or filter removed, or water in the petrol.

If the engine idles better after flooding (by depressing flooder-button) or when the choke is partially closed, the mixture is too weak. Conversely if idling is improved by temporarily turning off the petrol, and if there is no sign of spitting when the throttle is opened quickly with the engine cold, the mixture is too rich.

Trouble at quarter to three-quarter throttle opening is most likely due to wrong needle position. Very poor acceleration, but good power at full throttle, indicates too low a needle. Trouble at half to full throttle is probably due to faults at the main jet. Bad slow running will probably be due to air leaks.

For tuning, the throttle range is imagined as divided into four phases: idling (slightly open), running light (quarter open), general running (quarter to three-quarter open), and full power (three-quarter to wide open). The owner of a new cyclemotor seeking the best all-round performance should, as a general rule, avoid changing the main jet. The size of this has been carefully, and permanently, selected by the makers of the engine in consultation with the carburettor company (whether this is an Amal or another make) and it is a great mistake ever to alter it.

If a second-hand cyclemotor is bought, and the previous owner is suspected of having experimented with the main jet, then the best thing to do is to find out the correct size and fit this if it has been changed. With the needle, however, there is quite a different story, and it is wise to check the setting of this once the engine is thoroughly run in. Many engine makers purposely fit the needle one groove higher than is desirable for the fully "matured" power unit. When bearings are stiff and all parts fit tightly considerable extra heat is generated and the cooling effect of a rich mixture helps to prevent trouble.

It is simple to unscrew the top of the mixing chamber and then to withdraw the throttle-needle assembly. Nothing else need be disturbed, but the greatest care should be taken, as mentioned earlier in this chapter, to avoid bending the needle. Underneath the cable is a comparatively large and soft coil spring. If this is gently compressed into the hollow top through which the cable passes, the needle, with its retaining clip, can be drawn upwards and out.

The idea is to set the needle as low as possible—when of course it allows less petrol to pass—while keeping good acceleration and half-throttle running. If the engine spits back persistently during acceleration then the needle is probably too low. A cautionary word here: some spitting back and uneven running is to be expected with any engine when really cold, but these symptoms should disappear as it warms.

To reset the needle, slip off the spring clip and replace it in the next lower or higher groove. If the operation is to remove the extra richness imparted by the maker for the sake of a new engine, the clip is replaced in the next higher groove, when the needle will sit that much lower in the throttle. If persistent spitting back is the trouble and a richer mixture is desired, replace the clip one groove lower. The needle will then be raised by one groove when it is replaced.

Even the novice can perform this operation quite successfully, once the somewhat confusing effects of higher and lower are grasped—that the higher groove means a lower needle and vice versa. Never move the clip more than one groove at a time.

There are other operations with the needle-type carburettor, which are deliberately omitted here, such as changing the throttle itself. With a cyclemotor one would never do this, unless perhaps a second-hand cyclemotor has been bought in which the running suffers from a previous owner's unwise alterations to jets and throttle. In this case, if the parts are suspect, they should be returned to the makers with a note of the model and year of the cyclemotor and a request for replacement by the correct parts.

The foregoing contains all the hints and tips needed to obtain perfect, or near-perfect, carburation with the single-lever needle Amal. If they do not do the trick, it becomes necessary to check sizes with the makers as indicated.

The B Type Amal Carburettor. This has no needle in the throttle but two jets under the jet cap. Type numbers are 52, 352: 53, 353: 93: 103, 143. The initial 3 as before indicates a float-chamber lid secured by two screws instead of a screwed ring.

Petrol enters the float chamber through a needle port below the petrol-pipe union nut. It flows upward through a slanting orifice into the space sealed by the large hexagonal jet plug at the base of the mixing chamber. Here it rises through the two vertical jets screwed in from beneath and communicating with the air intake. The float keeps the fuel at a constant level above the orifices in the bases of these jets.

The main jet is the nearer to the mouth of the air intake, into which it protrudes. Its top can be seen from the outside when the throttle is raised. The pilot jet, directly behind the main jet, is slightly below the level of the air-intake and cannot be seen. When the throttle is nearly closed the bottom of the throttle barrel masks the main jet, which therefore remains inoperative. An air stream is allowed to pass over the recessed pilot jet, drawing petrol out of it and atomizing this.

The throttle barrel is cut away at a point immediately in front of the main jet, and as the throttle is opened this jet is gradually unmasked. Petrol is then drawn out of this jet and atomized in accordance with the effect of the cut-away. Eventually the throttle lifts above the main jet and this comes into full operation.

Its discharge and the airflow are then controlled by the speed of the engine and the diameter of the air intake.

As the main jet gradually enters into operation the suction on the pilot, being directly behind it in the air-stream, diminishes. The effect is to give a perfectly smooth change-over as the engine

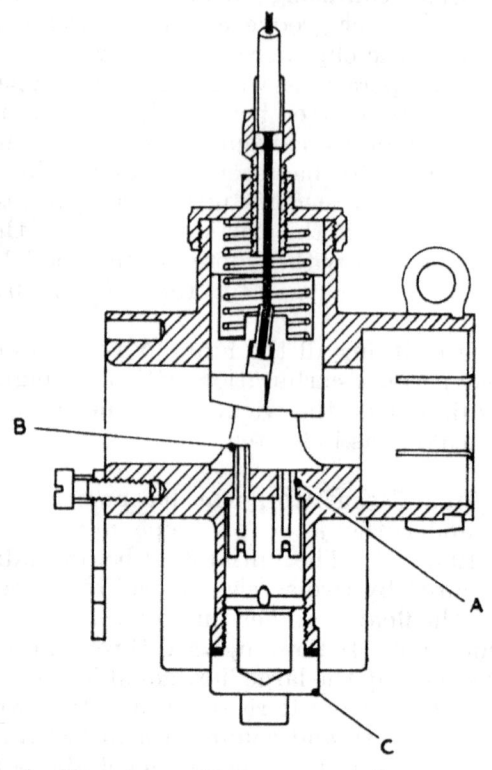

FIG. 6. THE AMAL NEEDLE-LESS CARBURETTOR
A. Pilot jet.   *B*. Main jet.   *C*. Jet plug.

speed rises. With this carburettor there is nothing to adjust owing to the absence of a needle.

Faults of running will, in the main, be confined to those arising from impurities in the fuel. Before any attempt is made to alter the settings of the carburettor, attention should be paid to the petrol passages, float chamber, float, and float needle (and of course to the ignition system).

From closed to quarter throttle the B type Amal operates on the pilot jet. This jet therefore only affects slow running and pulling. The smallest size is fitted which will give good idling while not affecting its correct blend, from quarter throttle and a

AMAL CYCLEMOTOR CARBURETTORS 23

little upwards, with the main jet. Hesitation and poor acceleration here may therefore indicate a pilot jet one size too small.

From quarter to five-eighths throttle the cut-away has the most effect on the mixture. Cut-aways vary from 0, which is flat bottom, to 5, cut-away $\frac{5}{16}$ in.

The main jet comes into effect from half to full throttle. Three variations in height are supplied by the makers, all having the same bore. The standard jet is $\frac{3}{4}$ in. long, overall. The greatest care is needed in removing and refitting either jet as the carburettor must be swivelled round before they can be seen. Loose jets will cause erratic running and they must be screwed completely home. Check also that the throttle closes properly.

It is most important with this type of carburettor to keep the petrol clean. The jets, being inverted, are not likely to choke readily and any foreign matter tends to fall down into the sump formed by the partly hollow jet plug nut. Whenever unstrained fuel is used, and otherwise from time to time as a general precaution, remove this nut to get rid of the dirt before it can be drawn up into the jets.

The strangler or choke is a simple swivel flap on the standard model, though a cowl or air cleaner may be sustituted. It should always be left open with a warm engine.

Much bad starting is caused by over-flooding, both with needle and needle-less types. Never depress the flooder button until petrol spurts from the carburettor. This is wasteful and messy, because two-stroke fuel leaves a film of oil when it evaporates. Experiment instead to find out exactly how much pressure on the button is needed to create conditions for an instant start. In general the moment to stop is when fuel starts to ooze past the button.

A small throttle-opening is also better when starting. This again can be determined with practice. Avoid stabbing or twisting at the throttle, which in most cases simply makes starting difficult. A two-stroke needs plenty of initial suction and a little time to draw the mixture into the sump, through the transfer port, and into the combustion chamber. This cannot happen properly if a wide throttle-opening is given. Listen for a sucking noise from the carburettor which tells that it is "breathing" properly as you pedal away.

CHAPTER V

THE "BANTAMAG" MAGNETO

"BANTAMAG" flywheel magnetos are standard equipment on the majority of cyclemotors. The "Bantamag," made by the Wico-Pacy Sales Corporation Ltd., of Bletchley, Bucks, is a small and extremely compact flywheel magneto based upon the simplest possible construction. There is a rotor, comprising the flywheel, a stator plate assembly, and a weatherproof cover.

Construction. The actual construction of the "Bantamag" is of "Mazak," a zinc base alloy, while the core is laminated soft iron.

FIG. 7. THE WICO-PACY "BANTAMAG"

The flywheel is a magnetic unit concentrating a powerful magnetic charge within a small space and volume. Because it can retain this high magnetic concentration indefinitely, the magneto retains an exceptionally high spark-output throughout its life.

On the stator plate are the coil and core, condenser and breaker mechanism and, when fitted, the lighting coils. All these are easily accessible for servicing.

The Bantamag is designed for engines up to 100 c.c. A size popular for the majority of cyclemotors of just under 50 c.c. is the model with a $4\frac{5}{16}$ in. flywheel and a weight of 2 lb. It is produced either with clockwise or anti-clockwise rotation to suit the engine manufacturer. There are smaller examples also, of which one typical magneto has a flywheel of 4⅛ in. and a weight of but 17 oz.

Adjusting the Breaker Gap. The breaker gap is the only adjustable part on the magneto. After removing the waterproof casing (held on by a spring clip), the flywheel should be turned until the contacts are visible through the flywheel aperture marked "set points 0·018 in. here." Caution: remove your wristwatch before touching this or any magneto, or you may ruin the watch.

The adjustable point is on an L-shaped base. Loosen the fixing screws just sufficiently to allow the base-plate to be raised or

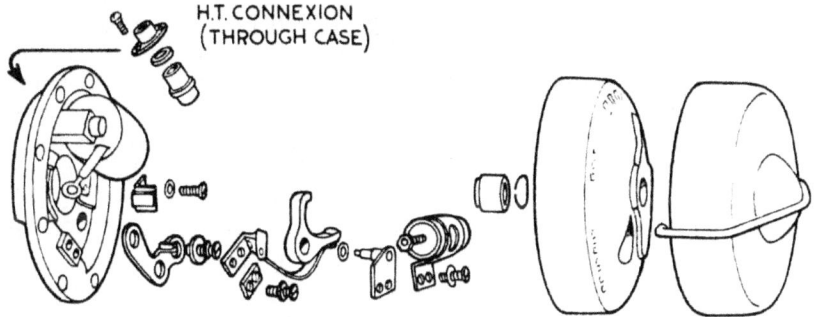

FIG. 8. THE WICO-PACY "BANTAMAG" GENERATOR (EXPLODED)
No lighting coils shown.

lowered. This is best done by placing the screwdriver tip between the raised edge of the stator and the breaker plate, either at the lower edge near the condenser or at the upper edge by the coil, and turning slightly.

Turning at the lower edge will lessen the gap; at the upper edge will increase it. Whichever you want, slip in, or close the gap on, your 0·018 feeler gauge. Tighten the mounting screws and test the blade for correct setting. It should only just slip out. Watch the movable point closely—use a spot torch on it—to make quite sure that you are not getting a false gap by springing the movable point.

It is impossible to carry out this operation properly if the mounting screws are too slack (or, for that matter, too tight). Also if the screws are withdrawn too far there is always a risk that they may fall out, with troublesome results.

The Contact Points. When these need replacement, it is advisable to replace both the fixed and moving points thus ensuring that they will close together properly. Do not oil or grease either the moving contact bearing or the cam surface. These are greased with the proper grade of lubricant at the works and should need no further attention throughout the life of the instrument.

If ever it becomes clear that the cam or the breaker-arm bearing have dried up, and you find it essential to re-grease, use the variety known as "high melting point." Apply no more than a pin's head of this, for grease wandering about in a magneto can play havoc.

To clean the points, press them together upon a proper polishing slip, obtainable from motor accessory stores, and rub gently back and forth till a uniform polish is obtained on each point. Doing them together in this way will do something to prevent their getting out of square.

If you cannot get a polishing slip (which is a slip of thin card like a nail file coated on either side with fine abrasive), wrap a slip of 00 emery paper, gritty side out, round a nail file or something stiffish of the same shape.

Brush all the debris away with a painter's small mop and just a drop or two of petrol if there is sticky dirt about. Have everything clean and dry before the cover goes back.

Should the points become bad enough to need refacing, as this cannot be done by hand, the best thing is to get a new pair. Get the old ones done up on a lathe and then carry them as emergency spares.

Tracing Troubles. If the engine seems dead and spark trouble is suspected, follow a routine before starting to strip the magneto. Take the h.t. lead off the plug and secure it somewhere to the outside of the frame or engine so that the brass tag is roughly $\frac{1}{8}$ in. from the nearest bare metal. Spin the engine fairly fast with the decompressor (if fitted) open. In a properly-performing magneto the spark should jump this gap.

If the engine misses at its highest speed, check the sparking plug. With this in good condition the magneto should fire a spark without missing with the h.t. lead $\frac{1}{16}$ in. from the plug terminal.

Generally speaking an easy start, followed by deterioration of performance up to maximum speed, indicates too small a magneto spark-gap. Too large a gap makes starting difficult but running is more or less normal at maximum speed. All flywheel magnetos are gap-sensitive and it is worth taking considerable trouble to keep the breaker points at 0·018 in. and the plug points a little more—generally 0·020 in. In particular cases these figures may vary, and the maker's instruction book is always the final guide.

Although the flywheel is not difficult to remove with the proper tools, or even, by an experienced mechanic, without them, the amateur is strongly recommended to leave it alone. Firstly, as soon as the flywheel is disturbed the timing is lost. Secondly,

THE "BANTAMAG" MAGNETO

it is more than possible to damage the end of the crankshaft during the withdrawal. Lastly, unless proper arrangements are made to fit a temporary keeper to the flywheel, its removal from the stator plate without due precaution can result in a serious loss of magnetism. This, unlike the current in a dynamo, cannot be regenerated in use.

The moral is for the amateur cyclemotorist to look after both sets of points carefully, but to leave more major operations to a service station. In fact the likelihood of professional services being required is remote.

CHAPTER VI

THE AUTO-MINOR (ABJ)

A. B. JACKSON (CYCLES) LTD.
300 Icknield Port Rd., Birmingham, 16

DESIGNED as part of a complete autocycle-type machine, the Auto-Minor engine is not sold separately from the A. B. Jackson cycle into which it is built. A two-stroke of 49 c.c., it is substantially "over-square," the 42 mm. bore being much larger than the stroke (36 mm.). The engine is mounted upon a pin fitting into the front fork crown. This provides a pivot upon which the engine is readily swung, from the free position, to drive the front tyre by a friction roller.

The die-cast flat-top piston has a floating gudgeon-pin held by circlips. Transverse flow porting directs the incoming fuel stream clear of contamination by outgoing exhaust gases. Cylinder head and crankcase are die-cast in DTD aluminium alloy, and a cast-iron barrel, spigoting deeply into the crankcase, is held between them by four long bolts. The head carries a decompressor.

The connecting rod, of stamped nickel steel, has a needle-roller big-end bearing. The crankshaft is drop-forged from carbon steel and carried on 17 mm. ball-bearings. It is extended to mount the friction drive roller and beyond this the Miller flywheel-magneto. At its outer end the crankshaft runs smoothly in needle-roller bearings.

The Carburettor. A bottom-feed Amal carburettor supplies a mixture of 1 part oil to 20 of petrol from the square half-gallon tank above the engine. As the air intake of the carburettor points upwards it is simple to operate the air flap while riding.

The Magneto. The Miller magneto includes the refinement of lighting coils. A 3-watt headlamp is positioned at the right side of the front forks and a rear light is, of course, also provided.

Enclosing the engine is a sheet-metal cover. The square front of this matches the appearance of the fuel tank and also provides a site for the transverse front number-plate. To the rear the engine cover tapers downwards with rather the effect of a roll-top desk. Only the bottom of the flywheel magneto on the off-side, and the exhaust pipe and silencer on the near-side, are visible with the cover in position. The fuel tank projects upwards immediately in front of the steering head with the filler cap just below the middle of the handlebars.

To the left of the tank the carburettor air flap is accessible with the cover in position. Olive green is the standard finish on the whole cycle, engine cover, and fuel tank, relieved by a neat gold name badge on each side of the tank. Equipment is complete, there being a sturdy rear carrier with number-plate and rear lamp attached, a touring bag at the rear of the large saddle, a chain

Fig. 9. The Auto-minor (ABJ)
Complete machine shown.

guard, and a centre stand. Other features appealing to the owner are internal expanding-brakes, substantial motor-cycle type of rubber handle-grips, and all-rubber pedals.

The short stroke of the engine makes it compact enough to carry fore and aft at the near-side of the forks, head pointing forward. The crankcase carries a drilled boss, and through this passes a slot-headed bolt to engage in a transverse drilling through the fork crown.

Upon the right-hand side of the crankcase there abuts, at the point of exit of the crankshaft, a cowling which three-quarter encloses the shaft extension and the carborundum-faced roller locked upon it. This cowling passes immediately behind the fork crown. At its right, or off-side end, there is located the magneto back-plate, and beyond it the flywheel, enclosed in the magneto cover. A boss, symmetrical with the crankcase boss, projects from the magneto backplate, and is similarly bolted to the fork crown.

At the base of the crankcase is another extension or boss. Through this passes a spring-loaded bolt. This slides in a slotted steel strip, the lower end of which is clipped securely half-way

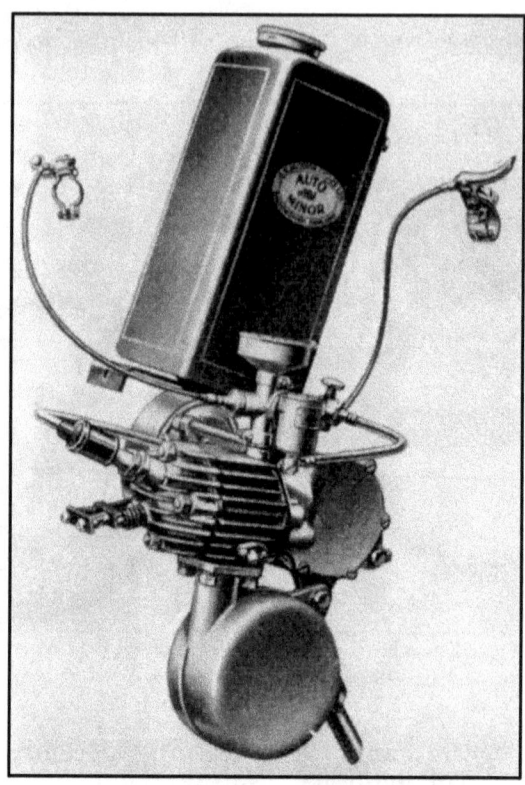

Fig. 10. The Auto-minor (ABJ)
Engine only shown.

down the near-side fork member. It comes up behind the roller cowling, and its purpose is to enable the engine to be set to "drive" or "free" positions. There is no quick way of doing this and the rider must dismount and take a spanner to the spring-loaded bolt.

The carburettor mounting is unusual in that the needle-type Amal is bolted direct to a very short vertical induction stub. Though the float chamber has naturally to be vertical also, the throttle barrel lies horizontally with the control cable emerging forward and the air cowl, as already mentioned, pointing straight up.

THE AUTO-MINOR (ABJ)   31

Exhaust discharge is correspondingly short, a drum-shaped expansion chamber being bolted to the downward-pointing port by a very short tangential stub ending in a suitable flange. The gases thus enter the drum at a tangent, and find their way out at the far side by an exit similarly tangential into a small-diameter pipe which directs them outwards and downwards. The design should result in the force of the gases being well spent without back pressure before they emerge into the air.

The 14 mm. Lodge plug is demountable and the ignition lead snaps on through a cap of insulating material. The Miller flywheel-magneto is highly accessible and to reach the contact-breaker points a circular plate retained by three screws is removed from the outside of the flywheel (there is no cover in the Miller instrument). The gap, it should be noted, is 0·015 in., a shade less than usual. Adjustment can be performed with a screwdriver and feeler gauge, as in similar rotating-magnet instruments, through an aperture in the flywheel. Once again a warning must be repeated that the operator should remove and place well clear of the field of the powerful magnet any wrist-watch or even pocket watch!

The direct lighting set, which works as long as the engine is running, takes 6-volt bulbs and the ½-amp. front bulb should give a good beam. The rear-lamp bulb takes 0·04 amp. and it is a good idea to carry a couple of spares for each. A battery is needed if a parking light is wanted.

The makers claim a maximum speed of 25 m.p.h. and there is no doubt that each gallon of "petroil" should yield more than 200 miles. The cycle is obtainable either with top tube (model AM) or open frame (AML).

CHAPTER VII

THE BERINI

Formerly distributed by MOTOR IMPORTS CO. LTD.
158 Stockwell Rd., London, S.W.9

WEIGHING $15\frac{1}{2}$ lb., the Berini is of Dutch origin, a two-stroke driving the front wheel by a friction roller carried on an extension of the crankshaft. The unit is of interest for two principal reasons. First, it is "over-square" in current language, since the bore is larger than the stroke (36 × 32 mm.). The capacity of the engine is 32 c.c. Second, the single-lever needle type Amal carburettor feeds the "petroil"-air mixture to the engine through a rotary valve. This is driven off the end of the crankshaft and helps to provide a smooth power output down to slow speeds.

The engine, inverted, is mounted on the right hand side of the front forks as viewed by the rider. A light-alloy crankcase and cylinder head are used, with a cast-iron barrel. The position of the engine and arrangement of the cooling fins should keep the head adquately cooled in all circumstances. To detach both barrel and head for decarbonizing, port cleaning, and inspection of piston and rings involves not much more than the removal of three long studs.

The drive to the front tyre is through a carborundum-faced roller held in contact with the tread by a spring. From this spring and its mounting a control goes to a handlebar lever by which the engine and roller can be lifted clear of the tyre at will, giving a declutching action. The other hand control, for the throttle, is on the right bar. No decompressor is fitted.

The Fuel. An egg-shaped tank is mounted centrally above the engine. It holds a third of a gallon of "petroil" in which the recommended proportions are 1 part of oil to 25 of petrol. The tank carries a reserve trap. When the fuel appears to be exhausted the cycle can be tipped forward, and the trap then empties enough into the main tank to get to the nearest garage. Petrol consumption is estimated at 240 m.p.g.

On the engine side of the forks are the silencer and exhaust pipe. They lie unobtrusively along the fork leg. On the left or near side a cowl, retained by a spring clip, encloses the rotating-magnet "Bantamag" magneto. The Berini is not supplied with provision for electric lighting from coils in the magneto.

THE BERINI

At first glance it might appear that the magneto is mounted on the off-side of the engine, since immediately behind the carburettor there is a cowl, retained by a spring clip, identical in appearance with that on the near side covering the "Bantamag." Also, from a point low down on the off-side cowl, there emerges the lead to the sparking plug.

In fact this cowl, fitted for the sake of neatness and symmetry, covers the end of the crankcase and the inlet from the carburettor

FIG. 11. THE BERINI

to the rotary valve. The sparking-plug lead is brought out of the magneto backplate and underneath the fuel tank.

The carburettor inlet is partly enclosed by the cowl, and the short pipe ends in a flanged twin-stud mounting on the side of the crankcase. The rotary-valve assembly itself is extremely simple. Turning on the end of the crank assembly are two washers. The first, nearer the crank, is a star-shaped spring keeper which maintains constant pressure upon the second. This is a disc in which a port is cut near the rim.

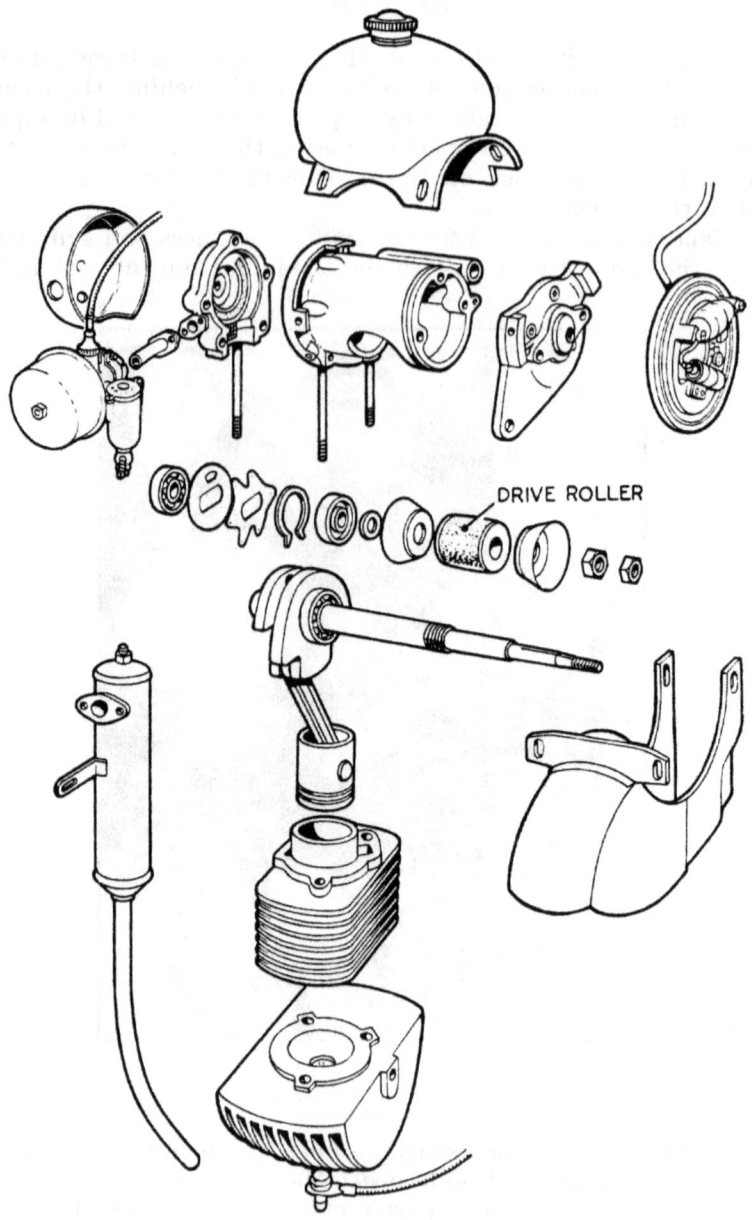

Fig. 12. The Berini (Exploded)
By courtesy of "Motor" (Holland).

THE BERINI

Pressed by the star washer it revolves against the annular surface of the crankcase surrounding the outer main bearing. For something like a fifth of each revolution it registers its port with a radial passage in the crankcase. This leads directly to the inlet from the carburettor.

Within the crankcase the gas takes the customary path through the transfer port to the combustion chamber. The piston has no deflector and incidentally carries two rings.

In more detail the mounting of the engine is at two points: a clip round the front fork bridge and a stay fastened just below the "Bantamag" to the near-side fork leg. This stay takes the reaction from the clutch lever operation and also from the spring-loaded drive. A neat pressed frame, also forming a replacement front-mudguard extension, carries the crankcase barrel.

The "petroil" tank has an integral curved saddle-fixing. This bolts to a cross-member at the front of the frame and to two short uprights at the back. The whole structure then gains considerable stiffness while still weighing very little.

Starting. For starting the clutch lever is lifted, bringing up the roller. The cycle is pedalled forward for two or three turns of the pedals. The roller is then lowered gently on to the tyre and after three or four revolutions the engine will fire.

Since no decompressor is fitted the rider must use care in bringing the stationary roller into contact with the moving tyre. The initial impulse to turn over a two-stroke should be applied progressively under compression. Failure to use reasonable gentleness in this respect is a main cause of uneven tyre wear. If one or two worn patches are formed on the tread by "bump-starting" these naturally tend to be self-aggravating and the roller will soon not have a smooth path on which to roll.

The rotary inlet-valve, which promotes good gas induction at all speeds, enables the Berini to run light without undue two-stroke "stutter" in moderate traffic. With the stop-start conditions obtaining in the central areas of most large towns it is, however, best to lift and stop the engine and simply use the machine as a pedal cycle until the road is clear. Also, with the engine stationary in traffic, overheating may well occur since the cooling is planned to take advantage of a stream of air.

Stopping the Engine. Since there is no other means of stopping the engine the throttle lever should be set so that the throttle completely closes. For hints on carburation the chapter on the Amal should be read.

The position of the Berini renders the air cowl or choke fully accessible from the saddle, indeed even when the machine is in motion. Thus though the choke should be closed when starting from cold, after a few seconds the rider will find that the choke can be reopened. In exceptionally cold weather no harm will be done if the air supply is kept shut off until the engine begins to lose power.

CHAPTER VIII

THE B.S.A. "WINGED WHEEL"

B.S.A. Cycles Ltd.
Birmingham, 11

The B.S.A. "Winged Wheel" is self-contained except for the fuel tank, and replaces the rear wheel of a normal bicycle. The tank, which takes half a gallon, is a thin flat structure meant to mount in the position of the rear carrier.

The Power Unit. A single cylinder two-stroke engine is used, "over-square" (36 × 34 mm., 35 c.c.) and mounted below the line of the hub with the cylinder horizontal and the head pointing forward. The cylinder is of cast iron and the head of aluminium alloy. These components are bolted to the crankcase by four long studs with nuts and saddle washers to bridge across four pairs of cooling fins.

The piston is of low-expansion silicon-aluminium alloy. It has a slight dome but no deflector, and the two rings are pegged. The gudgeon-pin floats within circlips and bears upon a phosphor-bronze small-end bush. The big-end is of single-row roller type running between the big-end eye and the crankpin, both of which are highly hardened and ground. There are two transfer openings, diametrically opposed and angled upwards.

Fuel and Performance. A "petroil" mixture of a strength of 1 part oil to 25 of petrol is supplied through normal induction and transfer ports. The performance of the "Winged Wheel" is that the engine has an output of one brake horse power and will propel cycle and rider at up to 25 m.p.h. Consumption of "petroil" mixture for this is at the rate of 200 m.p.g. The weight of the complete unit, including Dunlop Carrier tyre 26 × 1½ in., is 27 lb.

The Drive. The effort of the engine is transmitted through two pairs of gears, first to a three-plate clutch. From here it goes via the second pair of gears to the final drive pinion concentric with the rear spindle. The drive mechanism is concealed within what appears to be a large brake drum carrying the spoke heads round its flanged peripheries and having the engine built into its cover plate.

The Brake. In fact the term brake drum is correct, since the drum contains an internal expanding-brake of 9½ in. diameter. This, the makers state, gives a most exceptional stopping power and answers the criticism sometimes levelled against the cycle-motor-powered machine that its brakes may not be equal to its speed. An Eadie Coaster free-wheel for the pedalling gear is built

Fig. 13. The B.S.A. "Winged Wheel"

into the hub shell. Handlebar controls include three levers for throttle, clutch, and brake respectively.

Fitting the "Wheel." The width between the fork ends of the average cycle is 4½ in. and the B.S.A. "Winged Wheel" has been designed with this overall width between the off-side spindle locking-ring and the near-side aluminium-housing face. Slight variations in width, say ⅛ in. either way, can be taken care of by springing the fork ends. In a fork appreciably narrower it would

THE B.S.A. "WINGED WHEEL"

not be a good idea to try to fit the wheel. One wider could be accommodated by packing washers, provided enough spindle length remained protruding.

Fitting is extremely simple, the wheel being slid into position. With the pedalling chain in correct tension the spindle nuts are lightly tightened. Then the torque reaction clip is fastened over the chain stay, general alignment is checked, and the various nuts can be finally tightened.

The fuel tank goes on like an ordinary carrier, which as already indicated it also provides. When filling with "petroil" mixture for the first time care should be taken that no air-lock forms in the pipe from the tank tap to the carburettor union.

Fitting the Controls. A combined throttle-strangler lever is provided and this goes in the normal position on the right handlebar. As usual with this type of control, movement to the right operates the strangler and to the left the throttle. No decompressor is fitted.

The control for the powerful internal-expanding hub-brake should, the makers suggest, be fitted to the right handlebar. As the front-brake lever is normally fitted here this means transferring the front-brake control to the left handlebar, fitting it forward of the grip and in a roughly horizontal position (for reasons which will be explained in a moment). It is still desirable to get into the habit of using both brakes together, especially on wet roads.

Third of the controls, the clutch lever, must now be added to the left handlebar between the brake lever and the grip: hence the gap left when putting on the brake lever. It seems a little clumsy to have two levers to operate from the same grip, but in practice it is quite convenient as they are worked in two different planes. When all three levers are secured it remains to adjust them. There should be just a trace of loose or free movement on both clutch and brake controls, but the throttle-strangler lever ought not to have any free play at all.

Starting. The clutch lever has a locking ratchet which operates automatically when the lever is fully compressed towards the handlebar. Procedure in starting is thus to pedal away with the clutch disengaged. As soon as the bicycle is moving at above walking pace the rider squeezes the lever and touches the ratchet cam with the forefinger. Releasing the lever smoothly causes the clutch to engage and, other things being equal, the engine should fire at once.

Running-in. Considerable emphasis is laid by the makers upon the importance of going easy on the engine until at least 250 miles have been covered. In particular this refers to forcing the engine by sudden and sharp acceleration and by letting it labour up hill. In both cases heavy loads are imposed upon the new, close-fitting bearing surfaces.

Beneath the cover of the Wico-Pacy magneto there is a small drain screw projecting up into the crankcase. The makers advise that after 150 miles this screw should be removed, which will enable any surplus oil to drain out of the crankcase. Removing any such accumulation will also give a chance for foreign matter, collected by the oil, to come away at the same time.

The drain screw is also useful should an excess of rich mixture make starting difficult at any time, due say to over-use of the strangler in warm weather. If this screw is taken out and the engine rotated several times (the strangler being open and the sparking plug lead temporarily pulled away), then wet fuel and accumulated dirty oil will be blown clear of the crankcase. It is most important to replace the screw tightly to keep the crankcase airtight. The two-stroke absolutely depends upon this for proper working. A smear of graphite grease on the screw thread would be a good idea.

Overhaul after 1,000 Miles. Removal of the silencer and cleaning out of this and the exhaust port at 1,000–1,200 miles is advised. At double this mileage the cylinder head and piston should be cleaned. While this is done the gearcase, which holds one and a half tank measures, should be examined and topped up if necessary. SAE 50 oils, as for mixing with the petrol, are recommended.

The correct gap for the 14 mm. Champion 17 sparking plug is 0·015–0·018 in. Clean the plug and gap it very carefully each time the silencer is removed, or at each 1,000 miles. Another operation suitably carried out at this mileage is to clean the gauze "petroil" filter in the top of the float chamber of the carburettor.

After 5,000 Miles. Once every 5,000 miles remove the cover of the magneto and check the setting of the points at 0·018 in. If they look dirty clean with a little petrol.

Tyre Pressures. The rear tyre must be kept hard. Recommended pressures are from 40–55 lb. according to the rider's weight. One can get a tube with a Schrader valve so that the pressure can be checked with a gauge.

CHAPTER IX

THE CYCLAID

BRITISH SALMSON AERO ENGINES LTD.
76 Victoria St., London, S.W.1

A BELT final drive is used in the Cyclaid, a form of transmission which—at the time of writing—no other cyclemotor manufacturer employs, although the Mobylette autocycle has belt primary drive. As older readers will remember, at one time nearly all motor cycles were belt driven, using a vee belt and a large rear wheel pulley much like the present Cyclaid. Chain or shaft have superseded the belt on higher powered machines because no single belt could stand up to modern acceleration.

The British Salmson Company have, however, realized that the low power and limited acceleration of the cyclemotor render it particularly suited to belt drive. The belt has a natural "give" and the large pulley on the spokes of the rear wheel itself derives from them an additional resilience. Finally by mounting the engine itself under spring tension, the three points of resilience combine to produce an extremely smooth drive.

Mounting position for the Cyclaid is over the back wheel and the engine is suspended by a device which might be called a spring hinge. It cushions the transmission and also protects the power unit from heavy road shocks.

The Power Unit. Normal three-port two-stroke construction is used for the engine. It is "over-square" with the bore—35 mm.—larger than the stroke—32 mm.—and a capacity of 31 c.c. The weight is 14–15 lb. so that it is one of the lightest and most compact of cyclemotors.

The low weight is due to the use of aluminium alloy for all three parts: head, barrel, and crankcase. The barrel of course carries an inserted iron liner. Maximum power output of $\frac{7}{10}$ h.p. is produced at 3,500 r.p.m., a rather lower rate of turning than usual among small motors. This speed propels the cycle at 20 m.p.h. and gives a fuel consumption of 250 m.p.g.

The Fuel. "Petroil" mixture in the Cyclaid is weaker than usual, 1 part oil to 30 of petrol being recommended. A small Amal carburettor is positioned forward on the near-side of the engine. The choke or cold-starting control is readily accessible to the rider's left hand once the position of the intake has been learned.

Handlebar controls include a decompressor lever on the left, and—somewhat unusually—a twist-grip throttle of the same type as is usually fitted to a full-size motor cycle, occupying the right

FIG. 14. THE BRITISH SALMSON CYCLAID

hand position. There is no doubt that a twist-grip is extremely comfortable. One opens the throttle by rotating the grip inwards, that is anti-clockwise, and it is an entirely natural movement in slowing down to close it by turning the grip away from one with a pressure of the fingers. Twist-grips are fitted with a tension adjuster so that everyone can suit their own hand strength. The grip should just stay where it is set, but should turn back to shut at the lightest touch.

THE CYCLAID 43

The Cyclaid engine is carried by two mountings. At the rear an elongated stirrup is bolted to the rear wheel spindle by an extension nut. The engine rests at the top of this stirrup, upon a coil spring providing the resilient effect mentioned earlier. There

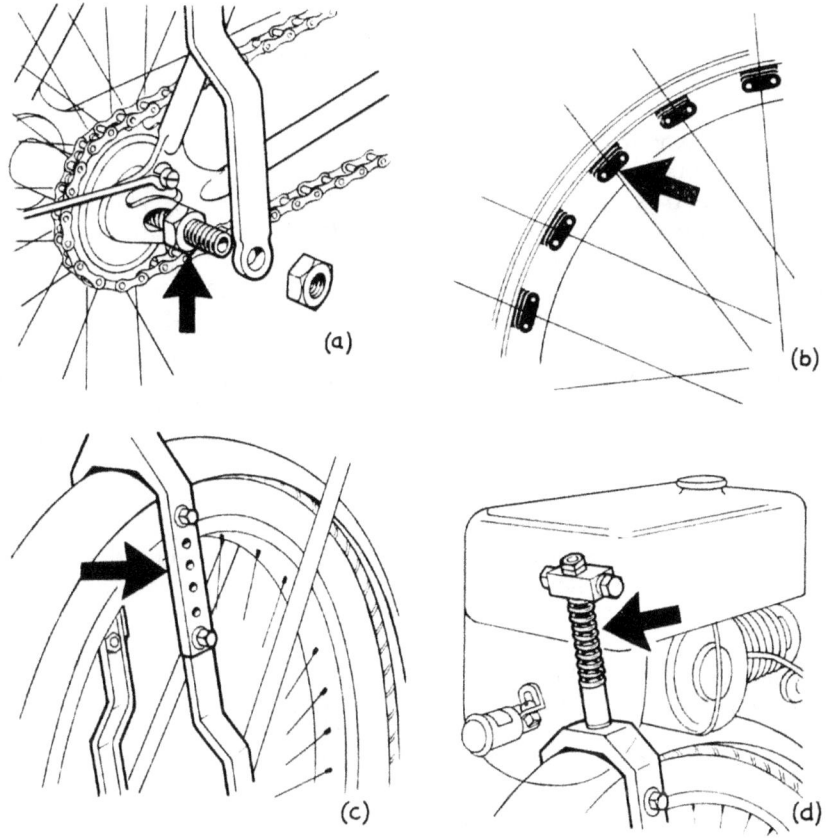

FIG. 15. THE CYCLAID
(a) Extension nut, rear spindle.
(b) Belt-wheel mounting.
(c) Adjustable strap.
(d) Coil-spring shock absorber.

is no provision for further movement as the Cyclaid does not have to be moved bodily from drive to free positions.

The frontal mounting is a double triangular pressing of considerable strength. It allows a flexing or hingeing movement which is limited by the rear coil spring. The front pressing is secured to the saddle-pillar by a heavyweight bolt replacing the standard cycle fitting.

The crankshaft drives a pulley, on the near or left side, through a helical gear giving a reduction of 1 to 3·7 at the pulley. The belt goes from this to a large, light vee-grooved rim bolted by screwed clips to the wheel spokes. The complete drive takes place on the near-side since of course the off-side is already occupied by the pedalling chain.

Between the two pulleys the drive undergoes a further reduction (1 to 5) so that the total gearing down amounts to 1 to 18·5. In other words the engine rotates eighteen and a half times to turn the rear wheel round once. This is a fairly considerable reduction but one which is clearly suited to the power unit.

As the belt wraps round the large pulley for some two-thirds of its circumference, the power is transmitted over the same amount of the pulley, since the belt draws tighter about the groove the more the engine pulls. This gives an additional flywheel effect, and as a result the Cyclaid will in fact pull evenly down to a walking pace.

At such low speeds it will not continue to two-stroke all the time. However, though it four-strokes—the "stutter" familiar with all two-stroke engines at low speeds—it still continues to run smoothly.

If at any time the rider wishes to pedal the machine, or if the fuel tank becomes empty, the stretch of the belt allows it to be slipped off the large pulley without difficulty. It should then be tied to the frame with insulating tape, well out of the way of the spokes. It should be left on the upper pulley.

Starting. This follows the usual drill of pedalling off (with the belt in position) on an open decompressor and a closed throttle. When the engine is revolving briskly the decompressor is closed and the throttle gradually opened. It is assumed of course that "petroil" is present, that this is reaching the carburettor, and, that if the weather is cold, the choke has been closed.

The fuel tank holds 3 pints and gives a range of about 110 miles. Petrol and oil should be mixed in a separate container and strained into the tank. The top of the tank forms a carrier and is fitted with strap lugs, while at the rear it extends downwards to make a place for the rear numbers or plate. A rear light is supplied, though unwired, there being no lighting coils in the "Bantamag" magneto.

CHAPTER X

THE CYCLEMASTER

CYCLEMASTER LTD.
38A St. George's Drive, London, S.W.1

SUPPLIED as a complete replacement rear wheel, the Cyclemaster engine is built into an enlarged hub. This, rotating round the stationary engine, creates a cooling airstream. The model is a two-stroke, of which early examples were "square," bore and stroke alike being 32 mm. and the capacity 25·7 c.c. These units can be visibly distinguished by their black finish with red line.

The Power Unit. Later Cyclemasters are "over-square" with 36 mm. bore and capacity 32 c.c. A metallic grey finish is used, and the flywheel magneto of the newer and larger engine incorporates a lighting coil.

The engine is one of the few with a rotary inlet valve, on the end of the crankshaft. This supplies a petroil mixture, using one part of oil in 25 of petrol, to the engine. Both models are fast-revving and will turn at 4,500 r.p.m., which should be treated as a maximum and will give a road speed of 20 m.p.h. The 25 c.c. engine develops 0·6 h.p. at 3,700 r.p.m., and the 32 c.c. 0·8 h.p. at the same speed.

Fuel consumption is some 230 m.p.g. The tank holds 2½ pints so that the rider has a range of about seventy-two miles between refills.

A normal plate-clutch is fitted and this can be locked in the free position. The makers state that a Cyclemaster-fitted machine can be ridden like an ordinary pedal cycle with the clutch thus locked and that there is no perceptible difference made by the engine weight. This alone—about 26 lb.—is no burden.

The Cyclemaster wheel is 26 in. with a 1½ in. rim. Fitted with a 1½ in. cushion tyre, this should be inflated to 45–50 lb. The same rim will take a 2 in. tyre, in which case the pressure required is less: 35–40 lb. With the Cyclemaster wheel is offered a "Mercury" bicycle built to match the unit in every respect, but sold without a rear wheel ready to take the Cyclemaster.

Dished towards the near side, the large deep hub containing the mechanism has eight radial ventilation apertures on the off side. At right angles, around the circumference, are eight groups of three transverse slots each, of which the fore edges are raised to trap air. This air, circulating internally all the time the machine is ridden, is constantly drawn in at the slots and expelled through the radial apertures.

The cylinder is carried high and canted forward a little. It transmits power to the clutch assembly, set below axle-spindle level. The clutch runs in oil and has a positive control at the left handlebar.

When engaged the clutch transmits the drive through a sprocket on the outer end of the clutch-shaft to a chain wheel inside the drum of the hub. Being completely enclosed within this on the off side, the Cyclemaster driving-chain is well protected from road dirt.

The only other control called for by the unit is a lever-throttle fixed to the right handlebar. No decompressor is fitted and the gradual engagement of the engine, when starting, is effected entirely through the clutch. Two separate cover plates enclose respectively the flywheel and clutch operating-lever (leading to the handlebar control) and the carburettor plate.

FIG. 16. THE CYCLE-MASTER

Through the lower of these plates there emerges the louvred intake of the carburettor (which can be closed, before the cycle is mounted, to shut off the air when starting from cold). Just above the carburettor intake is a push-pull knob (labelled) by which the fuel supply is turned on or off. The "petroil" tank is attached to the engine suspension-bracket and the lower part of the tank lines up with the higher part of the carburettor cover-plate.

The primary or clutch drive, enclosed in the left side of the lower cover plate, holds 50 c.c. of oil and is the subject of more detailed comment a little later. Controls and wiring emerge from the engine casting: the cable to the handlebar clutch-lever and —at the forepart of the casting—the ignition and lighting leads from the "Bantamag" magneto to the sparking plug and lamps.

Continuing the compact design the exhaust pipe sweeps outward from the engine to a flattened and curved silencer. This closely follows the underside of the clutch-casing and terminates in an exit pipe for the gases, taken well back.

The rotary inlet-valve is described by the makers as "simply a revolving disc of metal" on the end of the crankshaft. This disc has a port in it. At each revolution it uncovers a registering passage in the crankcase, to the outer end of which the carburettor is attached.

THE CYCLEMASTER

Each time the piston rises the rotary inlet-valve admits fuel to the crankcase. The Cyclemaster piston is not of the deflector type, but is domed, and there are two inlet-ports pointing upwards. The combined effect is that fuel entering the combustion chamber does not become contaminated with outgoing exhaust gases.

The carburettor is a needle-jet Amal with the feed to the base of the float chamber. Though it is completely concealed behind the cover plate it can be reached and detached in a few seconds.

FIG. 17. THE CYCLEMASTER

Using a screwdriver, first remove the air intake, and the single screw retaining the cover plate. The pinch-clamp, holding the carburettor to the inlet pipe, is then accessible for loosening with the screwdriver.

Starting. This is particularly simple. Pull out the knob of the "petroil" tap, allowing the fuel to pass, close the choke (if the engine is cold). Lift the clutch lever, mount the cycle, and ride away. Open the throttle by pulling the right-hand lever towards you, and gently release the clutch lever. After three or four revolutions the engine will fire.

It is not possible to ride too long with the choke closed as the engine will begin to lose power once warm. Disengage the clutch, dismount, and open the choke. If the engine has stopped it will now restart with the choke open.

After 150 Miles. A certain servicing procedure is recommended for the new Cyclemaster unit after 150 miles have been covered. The wheel does not have to be removed from the cycle for this service to be carried out (although wheel removal is quite simple). The owner can give this service check-over at home, although it would be a good idea to allow the dealer to attend to it.

The carburettor-filter choke and the cover plates are first removed. The plate bearing the "CM" symbol gives access to the clutch adjustment and the oil filler. It is held by a single screw.

FIG. 18. THE CYCLEMASTER AND "MERCURY" CYCLE

In the bottom right-hand corner of the clutch-casing an oil-filler plug will be found. Remove this and check that the oil level is no more than about three-quarters of an inch below the face of the filler-plug hole. If a screwdriver is inserted three-quarters of an inch the oil should just touch the tip of the blade. Over-filling with oil must be avoided. The correct grade of lubricant is SAE 140. If the housing is completely drained it takes 50 c.c. to refill, an amount exactly indicated by one fillercapful.

The clutch is likely to have bedded down. If there is no longer the necessary ¼ in. of free travel on the cable this can be put right at the routine adjuster where the cable enters the casing. When this adjuster is exhausted it can be reset to zero, and all the play taken up at the main screw and nut adjustment immediately beneath the magneto.

Having dealt with the clutch, check the wheel for alignment and at the same time make sure that the spokes are more or less in correct tension. To verify alignment, spin the wheel and check by eye that it runs true. If it does not, the amateur had better not interfere. As to the spokes, tap them lightly and examine with care any that do not ring. A little slackness can be drawn up with a spoke spanner. Anything worse, again, should be referred to the dealer; spoke tensions are highly important.

Much trouble can be avoided simply by keeping the Cyclemaster wheel clean. A periodical check on all nuts and bolts for tightness is thus rendered much easier. Especially observe the fastening of the frame fixing-bracket which, at the left side of the wheel, secures the engine bracket to the lower frame member.

There are a few jobs for an oilcan. Models up to No. 50,000 need oil-can lubrication of the free-wheel. Later models have an oiling point on the back-pedalling brake hub from which oil is also automatically taken to the free-wheel. The engine's driving chain, that is from the small clutch-shaft sprocket to the main sprocket, also requires a drop of oil. While the primary chain is lubricated from the engine the driving chain has no such supply. (Put a little on the pedal chain too while you are at it.)

Punctures should not be thought of apprehensively. If the machine is laid carefully on its right side the puncture can be coped with nine times out of ten. If the wheel does have to come out it is no more difficult than taking out an ordinary cycle rear wheel. Remember the frame engine-fixing bracket referred to a few lines earlier, which must be released.

All major engine attentions from decarbonization onwards call for preliminary wheel removal. The cylinder head cannot be taken off with the wheel in position. Detailed instructions and work sheets are issued by the Cyclemaster Company covering all overhaul operations.

CHAPTER XI

THE DUCATI "CUCCIOLO"

BRITAX (LONDON) LTD.
115–129 Carlton Vale, London, N.W.6

CYCLEMOTORS in general are two-strokes driving either the back or front wheel of the cycle through some form of extra transmission—friction roller, gears, additional chains, and so on. The Ducati "Cucciolo" is, at the time of writing these notes, radically different from its competitors in both respects. It uses a four-stroke engine and it drives the back wheel through the ordinary pedal chain.

It is also built into the cycle rather than attached to it, so that the machine becomes a lightweight motor-cycle rather than a motorized cycle. This impression is extended by the provision of a plate clutch embodying a pre-selector device for the simple two-speed gear. There is a positive neutral, obtained by pulling up and releasing the clutch-lever with the pedals of the cycle at "six o'clock," either being uppermost.

If the left-hand pedal is advanced horizontally—the "quarter to three" position—and the clutch lever pulled in and released, this gives low gear. If the right-hand pedal is advanced and the same procedure followed, high gear is engaged. It follows that the clutch must not be operated during pedalling or the gearbox will be damaged. But the gears are only changed when the clutch lever is pulled. The machine can be ridden indefinitely as a push-cycle with the gears in neutral and the clutch left alone. As the engine only weighs $17\frac{1}{2}$ lb. and is carried at the bottom bracket the rider will not notice its mass at all.

Some people are not happy with a gearbox but no visible and independent means of operation. To satisfy them the Britax concern is able to supply the "Cucciolo" with a gear lever at an extra charge of £1 1s.

Dealing first with the construction of the engine, this reveals more than one surprise. Being a four-stroke, it has valves, two of them, and they are both overhead—that is, they work downwards in the cylinder head, a system which gives livelier performance. Also they are operated by pull-rods, a system which the writer cannot recall in use on any other motor engine. It is rather a pity that the makers have left the valve gear exposed, since it must inevitably get very dirty. A pressed-aluminium cover held

THE DUCATI "CUCCIOLO"

by a clip would be quite sufficient to protect and neaten the job.

The light weight of the engine is due to the use of aluminium alloy for cylinder head, cylinder (linered) and crankcase. Bore and stroke are 39 × 40 mm., giving a capacity of 48 c.c. A relatively high compression ratio (6·24 to 1) and speed

Fig. 19. The Ducati "Cucciolo"

(5,200 r.p.m.) give the engine a power output of 1¼ h.p., so that one is left in no doubt about the abilities of the "Cucciolo."

A speed of 20–25 m.p.h. is recommended. Any higher speed, though it can be obtained by ingenious tinkering, is strongly deprecated by the makers. They rightly point out that a normal bicycle with unsprung frame is not built to travel at greater speeds.

Fuel Consumption. Provided the recommended speed range is observed a petrol consumption of 250–300 m.p.g. will be obtained.

Since the tank holds a ½ gallon this means that on one fill-up the rider has a radius of well over 100 miles. Since, by the way, the "Cucciolo" engine is a four-stroke, it has separate positive lubrication to the internal engine parts. A pint of oil is carried in the

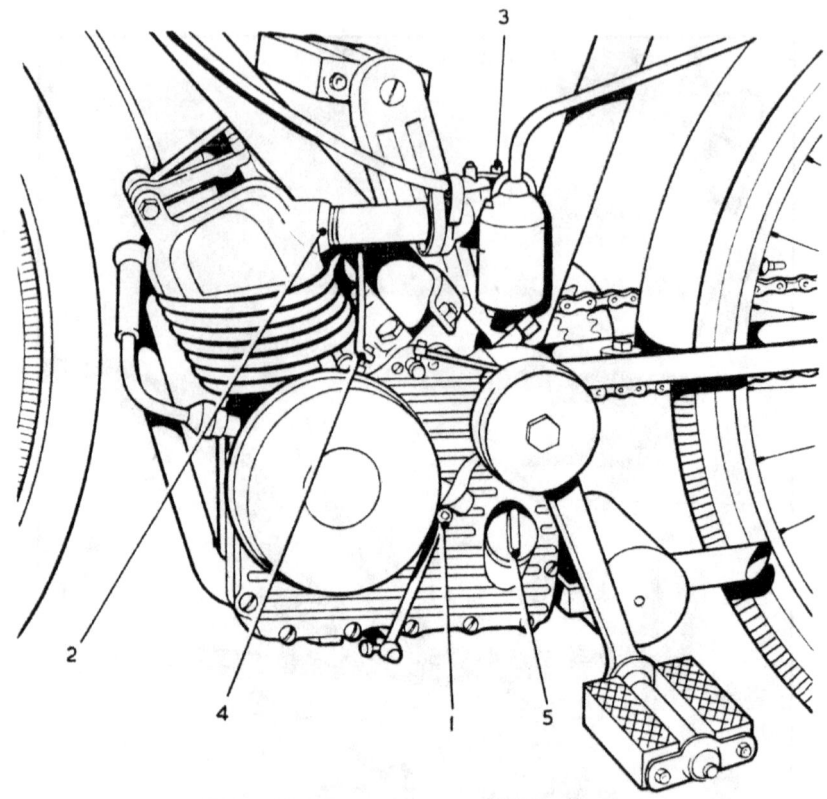

Fig. 20. The Ducati "Cucciolo"
1. Clutch adjuster.
2. Carburettor lock-ring.
3. Throttle cable lock-screw.
4. Headlamp terminal.
5. Oil filler.

Special attention should be paid to these points during assembly.

sump beneath the engine, and no lubricant is added to the petrol save for the upper-cylinder lubricant recommended during running in.

Fitting the engine is a process in which considerable care and mechanical skill is involved, although it is not intrinsically difficult. For this reason the workshop of the dealer is preferably sought rather than the limited resources of the amateur. If for

THE DUCATI "CUCCIOLO"

example the alignment of the engine is not correctly performed, or if the cycle frame, unnoticed, is not quite true, trouble will follow.

The engine is built into the bottom bracket assembly, the spindle, chain-wheel and right-hand crank being replaced by "Cucciolo" parts. A smaller sprocket is used and the chain must be shortened by a few links (a discouraging operation without a rivet extractor, but very easy with one!).

As the "Cucciolo" embodies a slip-sprocket it is better to replace the free-wheel, fitted as standard on most pedal cycles, with a fixed sprocket. If not, the braking effect of the engine on the over-run will be lost. Britax recommend alternative ratios for hilly or flat country and for the 28 in. and 26 in. wheels of British cycles.

A special Britax cycle can be supplied for the "Cucciolo" motor. This is built with an open frame, embodying fuel tank mounting and spring forks and it costs £18 18s. (purchase tax £3 12s. 9d. extra).

Since the drive is to the rear wheel sprocket it might be thought that advantage would derive from hub or derailleur variable gears. In fact this is not so, for the reasons given earlier condemning any attempt to raise the road speed unduly.

Ignition. A flywheel magneto is used embodying lighting coils and giving 15-watts at 6 volts, enough for a bright headlight and rearlight.

The carburettor is a Weber-Cucciolo 14 mm. instrument of the single-lever type with idling and main jets. Two gauze filters are fitted, one in the tank tap and the other in the carburettor itself.

Starting. This is performed in one of two ways, dependent upon whether the cycle is fitted with a fixed sprocket or retains the standard free-wheel. If there is a fixed sprocket the engine can be momentum-started. For this, neutral position in the gears is obtained and the rider pedals the cycle up to a speed of 3–4 m.p.h. Then the valve-lift trigger on the left handlebar is pulled up (this corresponds to a decompressor on a two-stroke), and the rider pauses with the right pedal forward.

This, it will be remembered, is the position to select top gear. Next, therefore, the clutch lever is fully pulled in and released. With top gear engaged the engine will start revolving, and immediately the rider releases the valve-lifter and opens the throttle slightly. Provided the petrol has been turned on, the engine will start at once. As the start is in top gear it is as well to pedal at first in order to help the engine.

With a free-wheel sprocket the engine must be kick-started. The same procedure as above is followed, starting in neutral, selecting top gear, lifting the exhaust valve, pulling in and releasing the clutch lever. Without again touching the clutch lever, advance the left pedal and thrust this down fairly vigorously to kick-start the engine, releasing the valve-lifter towards the end of the kick. Open the throttle, slightly above idling position. As the engine fires, help it with the pedals and open the throttle slowly to match engine revolutions to cycle road-speed.

No difficulty will be found about good gear changes if it is always borne in mind that when changing up, from bottom to top, the throttle is closed and not reopened until the clutch has been operated and released. When changing down, however, the throttle should be slightly but not fully closed, and it should be opened up again before the rider releases the clutch lever.

Running-in. A new 'Cucciolo' engine requires about 150 miles of running to free it, and this is just about what it will do on a full tank of fuel, if a speedometer or mileometer is not fitted. There is a reserve on the tank, operated simply by tilting the machine over to its left side, which gives enough petrol for another five to ten miles.

In fitting the unit, provision is made for the petrol tank to be located either astride the back mudguard, or, if a carrier is wanted, on the front down bar. With the engine new add a small quantity of upper-cylinder oil to the fuel. When run-in the makers say that it is unnecessary. But a trace will always keep the valve stems clean.

Changing the Oil. As the crankcase holds only a pint of oil the best economy is to change this every 500–700 miles. When new, and periodically thereafter, replace the drain plug and put in half a pint or so of flushing oil. Run the engine for a couple of minutes and then let it all drain thoroughly away. Refill with SAE 40/50 (summer) or SAE 30 (winter). Lubricate valve gear and control cables with a drop or two.

Adjustments after 1,000 miles. Every 1,000–1,500 miles reset the tappets: inlet to 0·006, exhaust to 0·008, both with the engine cold. At the same time turn aside the inspection cap on the flywheel and turn this until the contact-breaker points come into view. With piston at top dead centre the correct gap is unusually small: 0·01; however, the Champion L-10s 14 mm. sparking plug requires a gap of 0·018.

Adjusting the Carburettor. The carburettor has an adjustable pilot jet as on a large machine. One turn from "right home" is about correct. There is a throttle set-screw alongside it. Premium fuels will give best running. They will also postpone the need for decarbonization until 3,500–4,500 miles have been covered. This, as with any major overhaul, is best left to the "Cucciolo" dealer.

CHAPTER XII

THE ITOM

"Adimar"
26 Brixton Rd., London, S.W.9

ITALIAN-MADE, the Itom has a normal three-port, two-stroke engine driving through a reduction gear by a friction roller on the tyre. It is unusual, in that the purchaser is offered a choice of front or rear mounting. There is a slight difference in price due

Fig. 21. The Itom

to the recommendation that spring forks should be fitted for front mounting.

These forks, of link action, can also be bought separately, and they may also be fitted when the engine is carried over the rear tyre. They are complete with friction dampers.

The engine has a bore and stroke of 39 × 40 mm. giving a capacity of 48 c.c. Thus it is among the larger of the cyclemotors. Construction conforms to the usual three parts: cylinder head, barrel, and crankcase. All these are of aluminium alloy with a cast-iron liner in the cylinder barrel.

When fitted over the rear wheel an L-shaped attachment connects a light metal frame to the saddle-pillar at one end and to a stout stay at the other. The engine is carried under this frame in one of two positions, giving drive or free as is explained below. The L-member slides horizontally in a pinch-bolt clip on the saddle-pillar, and this provides fore and aft adjustment.

Another pinch-bolt clip at the end of the engine frame engages the downward half of the L, enabling the frame to be adjusted vertically. From one side of the engine frame clip a chromium-plated "crash bar" sweeps out and around the entire unit. This offers protection in case the cycle is knocked over. The rear stay-ends bolt under the spindle nuts.

The engine is attached, via the crankcase, only to the rear end of the frame. From the extremity of this a handle, resembling a gear lever, projects up towards the back. This gives the vertical adjustment mentioned above. When the handle takes the "up" position the engine is pivoted up so that the driving roller is brought away from the tyre. On moving the handle down the drive is engaged. In either position the engine is held by spring tension and this provides a shock-absorbing effect in the drive.

The Itom uses a decompressor controlled by the usual left-handlebar trigger. The position of the decompressor valve might cause it, if unshielded, to blow oil on to the rider's clothing. To divert any "blow-back" a pipe is fitted into the silencer.

A further refinement is found in the plastic cover to the sparking-plug terminal, combined with a quick-release plug cable. This protects the rider from possible contact with the plug while the engine is running. Similarly the plug is protected and cannot be impaired by external leakage, either from dirt on the insulator or water in wet weather.

The Fuel. The "petroil" lubrication is based on 1 part of oil mixed with 16 of petrol. A streamlined fuel-tank is carried on top of the engine mounting and connected to the Dellorto carburettor by a flexible pipe. The tank holds three pints of "petroil," consumption of which under traffic conditions is claimed to be 170 m.p.g. More than 200 m.p.g. would probably be obtained in running on the open road. The fuel tank is fitted with a lifting handle.

The Lighting. The rotating-magnet magneto includes 10-watt lighting coils, allowing front and rear lights of the direct type.

The "Tourist." This is a bottom-bracket-fitting model which is now being imported and its engine is basically the same as the rear-carrier model.

CHAPTER XIII

THE LOHMANN

BRITAX (LONDON) LTD.
115–129 Carlton Vale, London, N.W.6

INTRODUCED at the 1952 *Motor-Cycle & Cycle Show*, the Lohmann is a German development of considerable interest. In the first place it works upon the compression-ignition principle, familiar under the general name of the Diesel. When a charge of atomized fuel is compressed in the cylinder head (about twice as much as it is in an electrically-ignited internal combustion engine) the heat generated is enough to fire the charge.

Diesel-type Power Unit. The above is simply an attempt to explain, in general terms, how compression ignition works. Most Diesel vehicles use heavy-oil fuel, but the Lohmann, in all respects other than ignition and carburation, is an orthodox two-stroke using "petroil" fuel.

There is neither magneto nor sparking plug. Nor is there, in the accepted sense, a carburettor. Instead air is drawn in through a large air cleaner of tubular shape, and mixed with a spray of "petroil" in a simple pump. The charge is then blown into the crankcase by atmospheric pressure—or sucked in by the engine.

The Fuel. A mixture of 16 parts of commercial petrol and 1 part of SAE 50 oil is recommended as fuel. The grade of oil, 50, is relatively heavy and correspondingly takes a little more time to dissolve in the fuel. The "petroil" must be separately mixed and filtered in to the tank with particular care.

Although there could be substituted for the petrol other liquid fuels in which lubricant would dissolve, and although tests have shown that for a time at least the Lohmann will run quite well upon them, there is one deterrent to this. A heavy fine awaits the user caught and convicted of running his machine on any fuel which has not paid the appropriate duty!

It is not worth experimenting with fuels. On commercial "petroil" (there is no point in using "premium") the Lohmann will take the rider more than 300 miles for a gallon. There is no economy greater than this.

Size and Weight. Characteristic of the Lohmann are its extraordinarily small size and weight (only 11 lb.). Bore and stroke,

THE LOHMANN

28 × 30 mm., give a capacity of but 18 c.c., little more than a third of some of its competitors. No greater mistake could be made than to assume that its performance must match its size. It will turn over at 6,000 revs., a very high rotational speed at which it develops ¾ h.p. This is enough to propel cycle and rider at 20 m.p.h. on the level, and up a gradient of 1 in 8 unassisted.

FIG. 22. THE LOHMANN

The author picked up a Lohmann on the Britax stand at the *Earl's Court Show*, and held it comfortably on the palm and fingers of one hand. It is less than 4 in. wide so that it goes easily between the pedal cranks, it being a bottom-bracket fitment. It clips to the two bottom tubes through a resilient mounting. At the near-side rear of the engine a stay clips to the adjacent frame member.

The Drive. Behind the large flat plate, bearing the maker's emblem, that encloses the reduction gear, there is a short lever.

By this the drive is rocked in and out of engagement about the front suspension member.

The flat plate conceals a helical gear taking the power from one end of the crankshaft, through a 3 to 1 reduction, to a secondary shaft. On this is a fluted rubber roller driving the rear tyre.

The absence of magneto and carburettor, which helps to account for the low weight, gives the engine a very neat appearance. Almost the only projection is the tubular silencer slung horizontally beneath the cylinder, the head of which faces forward. The silencer mounting is light enough to be looked after by its coupling to the exhaust port. A short exhaust-pipe leads the gases past the rear tyre.

Another tubular component, almost precisely matching the silencer, is slung from the front of the front down tube. This is the air cleaner, always most important in a compression-ignition engine. A large-diameter rubber-type pipe leads directly to the crankcase at a point just to the rear of, and above, the cylinder head.

Between the rear down-tube and mudguard a third container, faired-in to the space it occupies, carries about a quart of "petroil" and is filled from the side. The flexible pipe from this enters the crankcase at a point just behind the swing mounting and near the air tube. It is within here that the atomizer-pump mixes air and "petroil" spray and passes it into the engine.

The Controls. The Lohmann is controlled by two twist-grips. The right hand grip, turned inwards, operates the throttle in the usual way. The left grip, twisted away from the rider, operates cables which, as can be seen, pass into the cylinder head beneath a plate secured by four bolts and bearing the maker's number plate. As the grip is turned outwards the top of the combustion chamber, within the head, is drawn up and away from the piston. This reduces the compression until, at the limit of leftwise twist, compression has disappeared altogether. In other words the machine can then be pedalled with the same effect as with an open decompressor.

When the grip is turned back towards the rider the movable combustion head approaches the piston. Soon a point is reached at which atmospheric pressure can force in a spray of fuel as the crankcase becomes exhausted. The mixture passes through the transfer as usual, up into the cylinder head, and soon the still-rising compression raises the temperature to flashpoint. The engine fires.

Full Compression. The figure is not available at the moment, but is probably something above 10 to 1 compared with an electrically-fired engine's compression ratio of some 6 to 1. After about 1,500 miles carbon formation will increase and still further raise the figure. Detonation or "pinking" then becomes noticeable—temporarily curable in the Lohmann by reducing the compression. The proper cure is, of course, decarbonization.

Cleaning Exhaust after 1,000 miles. It would probably be desirable to remove and clean out the exhaust before 1,500 miles have been covered. The air cleaner should come off at the same time for a flush-out with petrol and for re-oiling. The air cleaner should never be omitted, as a speck of grit in the fuel pump would put this out of action.

CHAPTER XIV

THE MINI-MOTOR

MINI-MOTOR (GT. BRITAIN) LTD.
Trojan Way, Croydon, Surrey

THE MINI-MOTOR is made by a company benefiting from considerable experience with two-stroke engines. It was one of the earliest, if not the first, of the cyclemotors to be placed on the market in this country. It is a straightforward two-stroke of 49·9 c.c. (38 × 44 mm. bore and stroke) with a flat-top piston, working upon the three-port system. It drives the back wheel by roller and is positioned behind the saddle.

The Fuel. "Petroil" mixture of 1 part oil to 20 of petrol is used. The tank holds 5 pints and there is an oil measure in the filler cap to ensure correct proportioning. Four measures are used with each 5 pints of fuel. The mixture, the makers stress, should be made up in a separate container before it is poured into the tank. Recommended oils of SAE 20 quality should be bought.

If at any time it is impossible to mix the "petroil" separately, the fuel tap should be shut and 4 measures of oil poured into the tank. Petrol is then added, the cap replaced, and the bicycle well shaken from side to side before opening the feed tap. This should be regarded only as an emergency procedure.

The Drive. With the original unit a cast-iron roller was used, and later the buyer had the option of a carborundum wheel. With the current Mini-Motor, however, the makers have evolved a hardened-steel roller of exclusive pattern. This roller can be fitted to earlier models. The off-side end of the crankshaft carries the roller, which drives at a point high up on the rear tyre.

The Mini-Motor is mounted in two places on the cycle. A bracket attached to the saddle pillar sustains it at the front. At the rear a stirrup, to which it is hinged and which is adjustable in various ways, supports it directly upon the rear-wheel spindle.

To Fit the Mini-Motor. The rear mudguard must be cut at a predetermined point. The rear piece is then moved backwards about its stay to allow the necessary clearance for the roller housing.

Fig. 23. The Mini-Motor (Underside View and Cut Away)

64   THE BOOK OF THE CYCLEMOTOR

Within this housing is incorporated a short mudguard, which closes the gap. Once the correct position has been found for the rear part of the guard it is bolted to the heavy-duty stirrup supporting the back of the motor unit.

Two clamps and two right-angle connections enable the front

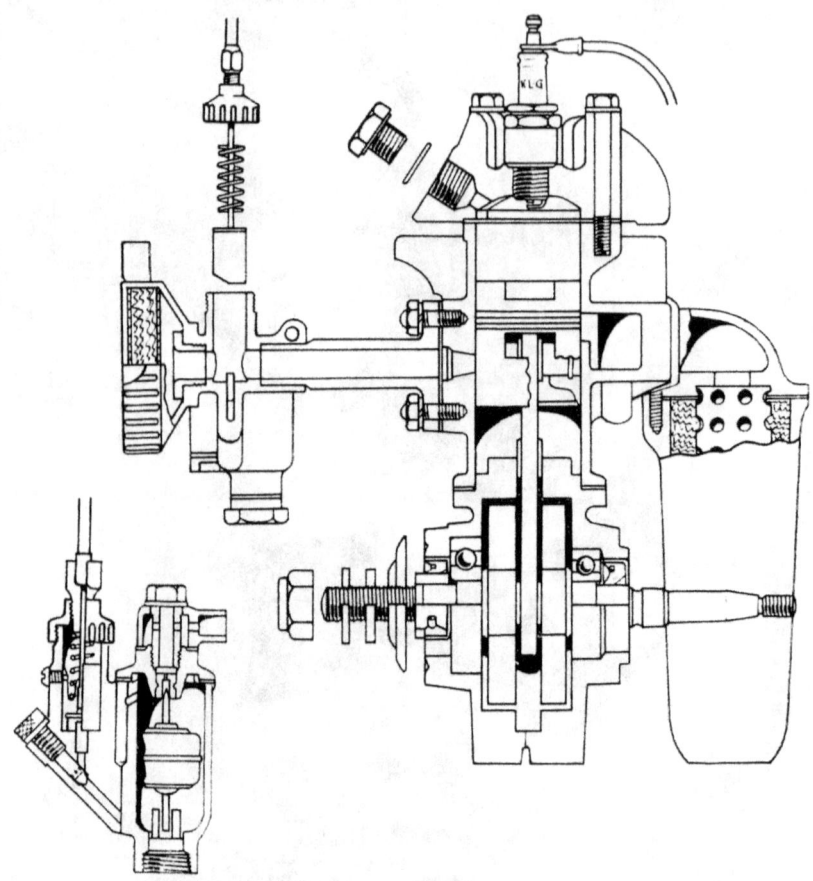

FIG. 24. THE MINI-MOTOR
Carburettor sectioned at left.

support of the engine, by which it is attached to the saddle tube, to be adjusted to the proper position. The tank top must be parallel to the rear-wheel spindle with the drive roller resting centrally on the tyre.

The rearward attachment of the engine is made between the off-side of the unit and the stirrup at a point some inches down the side member. Between stirrup and engine there is interposed a simple and robust spring-loaded adjuster. This works upon the scissors principle in conjunction with a long coil spring in compression.

The effect is to give a resilient mounting for the motor, cushioning the drive. At the same time means are provided by which the whole unit can be lifted clear of the tyre, allowing the cycle to be ridden by plain pedalling. Whichever position the motor takes up, with drive on or off, it is positively and rigidly secured there.

The Controls. A fixed-free control is operated by a lever on the left handlebar where one is accustomed to find the clutch lever on a machine so fitted. Resemblance to a clutch control now ceases, however, as the positions are reversed. When the lever is drawn towards the handlebar the cable to the scissors is shortened, drawing down the motor against the coil spring and bringing the roller against the tyre.

The handlebar-control lever locks on a ratchet in this position. When pulled closer still the ratchet is released and the lever will return to its outward position. The cable lengthens and the engine is raised from the tyre.

Another method of raising and lowering the engine is by a lever at the rear of the machine. If this is supplied the handlebar device and cable are not fitted. In this case the rider must dismount and raise or lower his cyclemotor from the rear. A special feature of the lever is that it can only be operated with a decompressor assembly fitted.

With the handlebar control no attempt should ever be made to start the engine by pedalling away and then drawing the unit down until the stationary roller comes into contact with the tyre. No matter how gently this is done the road wheel is liable to lock. If this happens the rider may be thrown from the machine.

The engine is carried horizontally at the off-side of the cycle, cylinder forward. The whole unit is housed in a rigid inverted cradle underneath the fuel tank. A single-lever Trojan-Dellorto carburettor is clamped to a short horizontal inlet-passage at the near-side immediately next to the roller housing.

This brings the carburettor intake, combining a mixture control and an air cleaner, a little below and to the rear of the saddle. The rider can reach it with his left hand without dismounting, an advantage when the carburettor has been set to RICH for starting from cold.

Starting. Throttle and decompressor controls are combined in a single lever on the right handlebar. As usual, pushing this away from the rider closes the throttle and opens the decompressor. For starting the procedure is to put the drive roller in contact with the tyre, turn on the fuel, if necessary slightly flood the carburettor, and close the mixture control or choke. The decompressor should be opened.

Pedal away and after three or four turns, with the engine smoothly revolving, move the right handlebar lever towards you. This closes the decompressor and opens the throttle and the engine can be expected to fire at once.

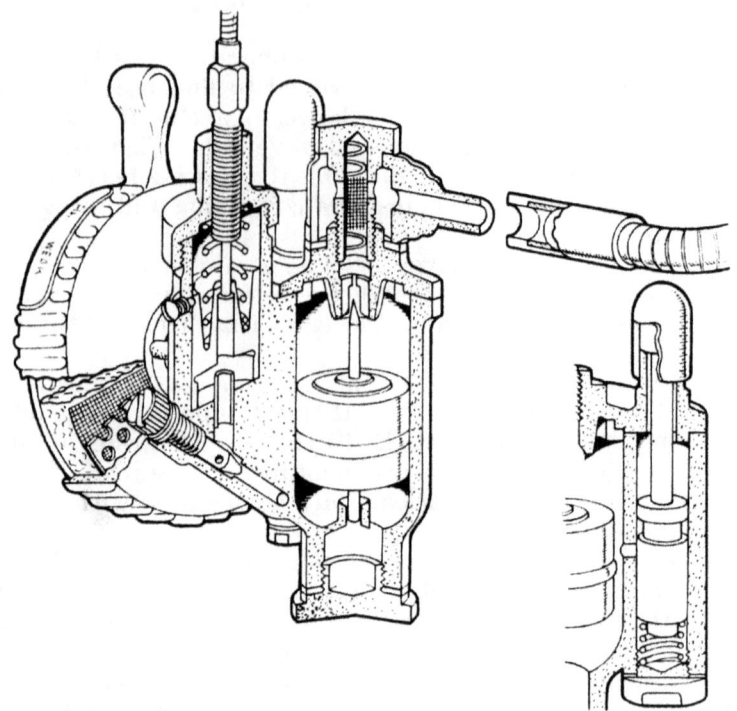

FIG. 25. THE MINI-MOTOR TROJAN-DELLORTO CARBURETTOR

Carburation. An interesting feature of the carburettor is disclosed in the words "mixture control" that have just been used. A limited but useful adjustment of mixture strength is available without dismantling the instrument. This compensates sufficiently for the difference between summer and winter conditions.

The external air-intake cowl is marked "RICH" and "WEAK." Arrows indicate movement, and, instead of simply shutting off or fully opening the air supply, one pushes the control knob in the direction of the appropriate arrow. For starting in cold weather it will need to be pushed fully to the right to give maximum richness. As the engine warms it can be brought back to the left

THE MINI-MOTOR

until full power and even two-stroking are achieved at all speeds —save the lowest—with the engine pulling.

Since the rider can reach this control with the left hand the object should be to weaken the mixture short of the point where the engine overheats. If a considerable variation in mixture strength is needed—say great climatic heat exchanged for severe cold—the jet itself may have to be changed.

There is only one jet in the carburettor. It is found beneath a screwed plug, set in an angle behind and to the right of the air cowl. If the screw is removed the jet can be pulled out with the fingers and cleaned or changed as needed. A No. 45 jet is standard.

Decarbonizing. Exhaust pipe and silencer form a one-piece structure bolted direct to the exhaust port by two studs and nuts at the off-side of, and directly underneath, the engine. A short piece of finned pipe is bolted by a right-angled flange to the absorption silencer. This can be taken apart when decarbonizing the engine after every 1,000 miles.

Three blind bolts hold the silencer to the flange. With these out and the parts separated the inner perforated tube can be withdrawn, together with the packing of steel wool between tube and casing. Remember to replace the steel wool when reassembling. Every trace of carbon must be removed from each part of the exhaust system, not forgetting the port itself.

For decarbonizing only, removal of the cylinder barrel is not necessary. When this is done two spare piston rings should be at hand in case of breakage, and also a new cylinder base gasket. When decarbonizing remove the decompressor valve, clean and re-seat if necessary. Screw it tightly back into the cylinder head, using a new copper-asbestos washer.

Every 1,000 miles. Mini-Motors are fitted with either a Wico or Miller magneto and in the latter case engine numbers bear the suffix Z. Contact points should be examined about every 1,000 miles and replaced if worn or pitted. Correct clearance is 0·018 in. with the piston at top dead centre. The same clearance is used for the sparking plug points. One drop of oil on the magneto contact-breaker-arm felt pad every 1,000 miles is ample—any more will cause trouble.

If the flywheel has to come off, never lever it from the magneto back-plate. A special withdrawal tool is obtainable from the Mini-Motor dealer.

The roller requires a clearance of $\frac{1}{8}$ in. when raised from the tyre. Early Mini-Motors can be fitted with the latest MA 161 hardened steel roller as fitted to the Mark III unit. Two other fittings which can be added to early models are the decompressor

(K 109) with or without a new cylinder head, and the positive toggle-lock for the back of the unit (K 107).

Enthusiasts completely stripping the engine (any model) should beware of overlooking or incorrectly refitting the oil-seals—one at each end of the crankcase. They are essential to maintain compression.

CHAPTER XV

THE MOBYLETTE

Motor Imports Co. Ltd.
158 Stockwell Rd., London, S.W.9

Designed and supplied only as a complete autocycle—the makers so describe it—the Mobylette is available in three models: standard, de luxe, and super de luxe. Common to all is the nearly "square" 49 c.c. two-stroke engine (1·535 × 1·645 in. bore and stroke, or 39 × 40 mm. approximately) fitted to a sturdy open

Fig. 26. The Mobylette Super de Luxe Model

frame just forward of the bottom bracket. Primary drive is transmitted by vee-belt to a countershaft, and thence to the rear wheel by chain at the near side of the machine. The overall gear ratio between engine and rear wheel thus calls for fourteen engine revolutions to produce one at the rear wheel.

The Power Unit. This is not sold separately from the machine, and is a two-stroke of straightforward design having a deflector-top piston. Since the use of these is now becoming rare, it may be helpful to explain that the deflector is a hump on top of the piston. The top of the transfer port enters the combustion chamber at right angles and without this hump the incoming mixture would be blown straight into the exhaust gases and much of it carried out through the exhaust port.

The steep, almost vertical side of the deflector in effect baffles the inlet port and the new mixture is deflected vertically upwards and sideways. The exhaust gas is swept out by swirl created by

Fig. 27. The Mobylette Standard Model

the more gradual slope of the deflector at the other side and so the two masses of gas do not intermingle to any extent. It is very important in assembling a deflector-engined two-stroke to get the piston right way round.

Aluminium alloy is used for the separate castings of the engine, an iron liner being pressed into the barrel. Just forward of the pedal chainwheel is the flywheel magneto and this incorporates lighting coils.

The Fuel. The tank of the Mobylette, carried between the saddle tube and the rear mudguard, holds just about half a gallon of "petroil," of which 12 parts of petrol are mixed with 1 of oil (French two-strokes in the main are designed for a rather oilier mixture than their British counterparts). The tank cap incorporates a measure to give the correct quantity of oil per tankful.

THE MOBYLETTE

(The temptation to mix the two in the tank should, however, be resisted—always mix and strain the fuel in, and from, a separate clean can.) It will do 200 miles on a gallon of fuel and its speed is 20 m.p.h.

The Controls. These are as follows: left handlebar, reversed brake lever for the rear brake and a small thumb-operated remote control for the choke—an unusual refinement on a low-powered machine. Right handlebar, reversed (front wheel) brake lever and a twist grip of orthodox motor-cycle type. Twisted away from the rider and past the closed position it operates the decompressor. Twisted towards the rider it opens the throttle. Another control, not on the handlebars but on the pedal pulley (at the near-side) disengages the back wheel from the engine. A knurled spring-loaded plunger is merely pulled out of an inner and brought back into an outer socket. The Mobylette can then be ridden as a pedal cycle.

The de luxe and super models have a novel feature possibly unique on a bicycle: an automatic centrifugal clutch operated by cycle speed. It engages without action from the rider other than that of pedalling up to a brisk walking pace. When the machine slows down to this speed again the drive is automatically disconnected. If the throttle is set suitably the engine will continue to tick over with the cycle stationary.

The Brakes. Standard and de luxe models have normal cycle front forks. The two rim brakes of the standard model become a front rim and an internal-expanding rear hub-brake in the de luxe. The super model has two internal-expanding brakes and telescopic front-forks. Large white cushion tyres (600.50B special) give an attractive appearance to all models.

Frame colours are in beige or gunmetal and, as well as reversed brake levers, there is a neat and partial concealment of control cables within the frame tubes.

The total weight of the Mobylette is 65 lb. The machines, which are French, come from the well-known Motobécane motor-cycle manufacturing concern.

CHAPTER XVI

THE MOCYC

CAIRNS CYCLE & ACCESSORY MFG. CO. LTD.
Stoneswood, Todmorden, Lancs.

SUPPLIED either complete with a cycle of the maker's own or as a separate unit, the Cairns Mocyc is a straightforward two-stroke of 49 c.c. (39 × 42 mm. bore and stroke). It weighs approximately 20 lb. and drives direct on the front tyre by a carborundum-faced

FIG. 28. THE MOCYC

roller. It is carried on a cradle formed by two tubes clamped at their upper ends to the handlebars and at the lower extremities under the front-spindle nuts. Extension parts are fitted for this.

The Power Unit. The engine, of aluminium throughout save for the internal components, has a separate cylinder and detachable head. Liner, deflector piston, and rings are of Wellworthy make. A single-lever Amal carburettor supplies a 1 to 16 oil-petrol mixture which the 14 mm. Champion plug fires by a Wico-Pacy "Bantamag."

A single engine control fitted to the right handlebar operates a decompressor when pushed to the right and the throttle on the left-hand range. Up to 225 m.p.g. is claimed at a road speed of 18–20 m.p.h. The tank, fitted above the engine, holds a $\frac{1}{3}$ gallon, giving a range of 75 miles.

The engine is hinged in the cradle, enabling it to be swung clear of the front tyre and so disengaged if the machine is to be ridden like an ordinary bicycle. The only permanent alteration to the cycle in fitting involves the removal of all but 2 in. of the front mudguard extension, to clear the driving roller.

Bolted direct to the exhaust port, the silencer is carried vertically forward at the off-side of the engine. There are four securing bolts, the upper two at the level of the port and the lower pair fastening the silencer at the centre of its body to the crankcase. The exhaust pipe extends downwards nearly to the front spindle.

Starting. For starting, the engine is moved into the drive position. Fuel is turned on and, if working from cold, the choke is closed. The decompressor is opened by pushing the handlebar control to the right and the cycle is pedalled up to a brisk walking pace. Moving the right hand lever leftwards, to close the decompressor and open the throttle, will then get the engine firing.

As the carburettor is accessible from the saddle, at the left side of the engine, the rider can partially open the choke as soon as the machine is running. When even running is obtained the choke should be opened until the full air supply is admitted. It is emphasized that a new engine should always be assisted by light pedalling, especially to help it on hills.

Adjustments after Running-in. After 100 miles of running all the engine bolts will need some tightening to take up settlement. At 250 miles, and thereafter at 500 and so on, the sparking plug should be unscrewed from the engine and cleaned. When fully run-in the plug will appear greyish with clean points if the mixture is correct. At the first 250 miles or maybe before it will be desirable to clean and dismantle the carburettor as well.

The instrument is supplied new with a No. 27 main jet. It may be found after thorough running-in that this can be advantageously changed for a No. 25, especially if there is persistent four-stroking. Do not, however, hasten to change the main jet until all other maintenance points have been checked over first.

Cleaning the Exhaust Port and Silencer. It is most important to keep the exhaust port and silencer clean and this can well receive attention every few hundred miles. It is simple to take the exhaust system off by removing the four holding bolts. The tail piece of the silencer is held by a securing bolt and is easily removed.

Decarbonizing. It is unlikely that, with skilful and progressive running-in, the engine, at its first decarbonizing, will need to be stripped beyond lifting the cylinder head and the removal and cleaning of the silencer and exhaust port.

CHAPTER XVII

THE MOSQUITO

Mosquito Motors Ltd.
Moorfields, Liverpool, 2

FITTED to the bottom bracket of any cycle in thirty minutes, the Mosquito is a 35 × 40 mm. two-stroke of 38·5 c.c., weighing 15 lb. It drives the back tyre by a large ribbed roller of metal, to which power is delivered through a 2 to 1 reduction gear.

The Fuel and Performance. Maximum speed is 20 m.p.h., at which the engine is turning at 4,200 r.p.m. The makers claim that it will take an adult up a gradient of 1 in 10 without pedalling, and 1 in 5–6 with some pedalling. Using the recommended proportions of 1 to 16, oil to petrol, consumption is stated to be at least 250 m.p.g.

The Mounting. Garelli of Milan make the engine, which is particularly simple to fit. It is carried beneath the bottom bracket, a clamp held by one bolt passing between the rear fork-tubes. At the front of the engine is a flat strip of spring steel which bolts to a clip round the front down-tube.

This method of attachment allows the engine to be moved bodily back and forth about an inch, and a small lever on the near side controls this movement. It is enough to bring the unit into or out of contact with the rear wheel. The steel strip also ensures that the roller is in constant spring tension against the tyre. The overall width, just under 4 in., is small enough to clear both pedal cranks. If the engine is pushed out of contact with the tyre, the cycle can be ridden as if the motor were not there.

Roller bearings are used for the crankshaft and needle rollers for the large connecting-rod bearing. The driving roller serves an ingenious dual purpose. It is twice the size usually associated with this component, and mounted on ball bearings. Within it are the rotating magnets of the magneto.

The stationary coil lead is brought out through the crankcase casting. The high-tension pickup, a spring-loaded bush, is pressed into the crankcase face by four screws and thus kept against a carbon contact within the coils. This eliminates all the usual external magneto mounting.

Light alloy is used for the detachable cylinder head, the

crankcase and the casing of the 2 to 1 reduction gear. This casing, like the engine, is generously ribbed for cooling.

The cylinder itself, and the three ring piston, are made of light cast iron of the variety known as "Perlitic." By making these two components of the same hard-wearing material, piston-cylinder troubles should be reduced to a minimum.

Porting is of the usual inlet-transfer-exhaust variety, the ports being inclined so as to deflect incoming mixture from the exhaust

Fig. 29. The Mosquito

gases. There is no deflector on the piston, the crown of which is slightly domed. A single exhaust port leads away to a flattened expansion chamber which fits inconspicuously under the engine. From this an exhaust pipe protrudes horizontally to the rear.

Carburation. This is by a single-jet Dellorto. Though very small, 10 mm., its jet can be removed for cleaning by taking out a single screw. There is no need to drain the instrument while so doing. The air filter and choke, combined, face forward, but the actual intake is to the rear. A drip tray leads any overflow of fuel clear of the engine.

The flooder or tickler does not actuate the float and disturb the needle. Instead, depressing the button operates an extremely small suction pump. This forces fuel up into the mixing chamber.

THE MOSQUITO

When released a fresh charge of fuel, ready for next time, is drawn from the float chamber.

Fuel is carried either in a flat half-gallon tank combined with a rear carrier and slung underneath it, or in a smaller cylindrical tank secured beneath the saddle. A flexible pipe feeds the carburettor and the half-gallon tank provides a range of some 125 miles.

Starting. Control is simple. Two levers, a normal throttle trigger and one for the decompressor, are fitted to a common clamp on the right handlebar. The usual starting procedure is followed: fuel is turned on, the decompressor opened, and with the roller on the tyre one pedals away for four or five strokes. Then the decompressor is closed and the throttle opened. Normally the engine will fire at once.

The contact-breaker is in a housing on the off or right side of the engine. The breaker itself is worked by a cam on the crankshaft. The cover is masked by the cycle chainwheel but as the whole engine can be lowered in a few minutes, by undoing the two retaining bolts, no hardship really ensues when the points require adjustment or cleaning.

The Drive. The gear drive, totally enclosed within its aluminium housing, is lubricated by grease. The primary drive is through a helical gearwheel riveted to the inner face of the flywheel. This is exposed at the off-side of the engine.

Tyre Maintenance. The tyre should be kept inflated hard. With the motor in the disengaged position the gap between roller and tyre should be no more than $\frac{1}{8}$ in. If it varies this can generally be taken as a sign that the spring tension requires adjustment. Mosquito Motors state that if these three simple points are carefully observed there will be no tyre wear due to the roller, no slip in the drive, wet or dry, and general all-round satisfaction. Unfortunately the average British bicycle rider can rarely be persuaded to check his tyres, perhaps because the Woods valve prevents a pressure gauge being used.

Engine Failures. Gradual deterioration of the ignition due to neglect is the commonest cause of two-stroke failures. Therefore the Mosquito makers urge regular attention to the contact-breaker and plug points.

Preventing Failures. The comparatively fierce spark of the flywheel-type magneto erodes the plug points more rapidly than in the case of a car or a four-stroke motor cycle with coil or rotating-armature ignition. The centre electrode becomes pitted at the extremity. Thus after considerable use a plug may at a glance appear to have the correct gap. In fact as a stepped piece has been eaten out of the centre electrode the gap may be three times what it should be. The remedy, if the plug is detachable, is to remove the core and most carefully grind or file away the "bitten end." But not too much or the firing points may become masked. About 0·02 in., the thickness of one's thumbnail, is a good gap.

The contact-breaker gap should be smaller, 0·015–0·018 in., and it is fairly critical. These points do the opposite to the plug—they narrow because the fibre cam slowly wears down and this is equivalent to closing the gap. Probably for 2,000 miles the gap will be restored to its correct figure simply by burnishing the points, as they become burnt or discoloured, with grades 0 or 00 emery paper or cloth wrapped round a thin slip. Press gently down on the moving point while sliding the slip to and fro between them. When bright, clean the minute specks of emery from the points by wiping with a soft scrap of rag damped with petrol. An unremoved speck of emery still on the surface of the points can effectively prevent the engine starting.

At 700 miles. Another way of forestalling trouble, mentioned more than once in these pages, is to clean the "petroil" filters regularly. Make up the "petroil" in a clean, separate container, using good quality oil of the right viscosity. Clear carbon from the silencer, exhaust port, piston crown, and cylinder head every 600–700 miles. If in a hurry, the silencer and exhaust port are the more important.

After 2,000 Miles. Every 2,000 miles draw off the cylinder barrel and give a thorough decarbonization. This includes getting out carbon from behind the piston rings (it is well to have spares for piston rings break more easily than teacups) and from the inside of the piston. Try to remember to leave a skin of carbon round the top "land"—the area between the uppermost ring and the crown of the piston.

After 3,000 Miles. Between 3,000–4,000 miles take off the flywheel (or get a Mosquito agent to do it), swab out all the old grease with a cheap long-bristled paintbrush and half a pint of paraffin, and when dry re-cover the gear teeth with a new coating of grease. There are various grades for gears. In replacing the flywheel the engine must be retimed, which is not difficult with the aid of the instruction book.

Stripping the Engine. At any time when doing this beware of tampering with the two deflector plugs protruding from either side

THE MOSQUITO

of the barrel. They are pressed in to cover the machining of the ports during manufacture and should not be removed or turned.

Alternative Forks. With the Mosquito there can also be supplied an Italian-built girder spring fork, the "Alfa." It is only $2\frac{1}{2}$ lb. heavier than the rigid cycle fork and can be fitted to any cycle of 21, 22, or 23 in. frame (irrespective of whether a cyclemotor is used or not). The lengths of the "Alfa" steering stem to suit frame sizes are $7\frac{1}{4}$, $8\frac{1}{2}$, or $9\frac{1}{4}$ in.

It closely resembles the girder forks formerly fitted to all larger motor cycles. Grease nipples are fitted to all spindles and the lower outer link has adjustable dampers. The check spring is chromium plated. A spring fork makes a great difference to the rider's comfort if much mileage over rough roads is contemplated.

CHAPTER XVIII

THE POWER PAK

SINCLAIR GODDARD & CO. LTD.
162 Queensway, London, W.2

FITTED over the back wheel of the cycle, the Power Pak auxiliary is basically a simple and orthodox two-port two-stroke (39 × 41 mm., 49 c.c.) with a deflector piston. A 16 to 1 petrol to oil mixture is specified and is claimed to give at least 200 m.p.g. The whole unit, with fuel tank and fittings, weighs 22 lb.

The Drive. This is to the rear tyre through a ribbed roller of special steel, in the making of which more than usual care is taken. Contending that a roller drive should not, if properly designed and fitted, cause any more wear to the tyre than occurs on the undriven wheel, the makers bring several interesting theories to bear.

The first is that the drive should be rigid to eliminate all slip. The Power Pak unit is thus positively locked in both the free and drive positions and the only resilience permitted is that between tyre and roller.

In the second place the ribs on the roller are profiled to suit and match the tread of one particular tyre, a cover designed by the Dunlop company expressly for cyclemotors with roller drive. One of these covers is included in the purchase price of all Power Pak models.

Though the drive is rigid, apart from the give in the inflated cover, the whole motor is mounted at two points on a rubber suspension which insulates the cycle frame from vibration. A platform like any ordinary robust cycle rear-carrier is secured at the fore end, through a rubber sandwich, to the down stays beneath the saddle.

At the rear this platform is linked by a U-shaped rod to a rubber-bushed stay extending down to, and retained under, the off-side spindle nut. The outer end of the platform terminates in a useful lifting handle.

The fuel tank is carried above this platform, from underneath which the engine is in effect hung, upside down, at the off-side of the rear wheel. The positive lock in "drive" or "free" is secured by a simple hinge arrangement working through a lever just below the saddle at the near-side.

THE POWER PAK

In the upper notch the engine is held with an $\frac{1}{8}$ in. clearance between roller and tyre. In the lower it is brought down, in effect, about $\frac{1}{4}$ in. and the grooves and ribs in the roller mesh with the tread of the cover at a predetermined pressure—assuming always that the rider does his part in keeping the tyre properly

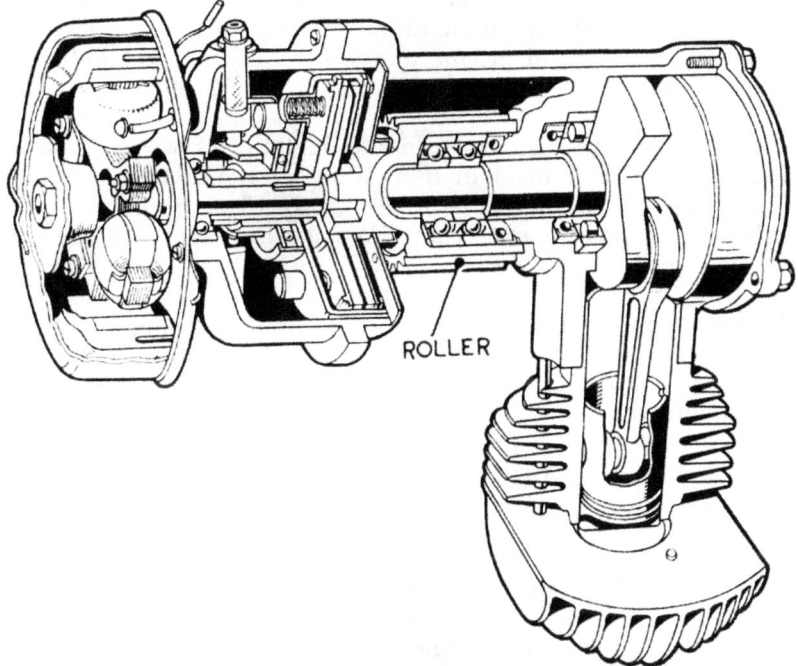

FIG. 30. THE POWER PAK WITH SYNCHROMATIC DRIVE
(CUT AWAY)
The clutch is to the left of the roller.

inflated. The importance of this, is incidentally, a matter of constant emphasis by the makers.

To Fit the Power Pak. The rear mudguard must be cut through and the hind part rotated rearwards to make a 4 in. gap. Fitting is otherwise very simple provided the utmost care is given at all stages to alignment. Thus the roller must be dead square with the tyre and the specified $\frac{1}{8}$ in. clearance is highly important. It can be accurately determined either by using the gauge set provided, or by inserting as a distance piece two new halfpennies one on top of the other.

The Fuel. The fuel tank includes an oil measure in the cap. It will take the $\frac{1}{2}$ gallon of petrol *and* the $\frac{1}{4}$ pint of oil called for, though the wiser user will resist the temptation to try to get a proper "petroil" mixture in the tank. Separate, thorough mixing in a scrupulously clean container, and the use of a fine-mesh strainer, will save many troublesome occasions on the road. The full tank gives a cruising range of 100 miles.

As the tank occupies the position usually taken by a rear carrier, the Power Pak makers can supply as an extra a large enamel or chrome grid, fitting above the tank. It is rigidly held at three fixing points.

The Power Unit. Engine details include a two-ring piston, detachable cylinder head in light alloy and similar material for the crankcase. The barrel is of cast iron. Close finning of barrel and head supports the maker's claim that the engine will not overheat even in hot climates.

Ignition and Carburation. Ignition is by "Bantamag" flywheel magneto and a 14 mm. sparking plug. The carburettor is a needle-type Amal. The simpler model Power Pak has a decompressor and a two-cable "fingertip" control which is the only fitment on the handlebars extra to the cycle brakes. The control can be mounted equally well on either handlebar, a useful point for the left-handed. The model is now available with twist-grip control.

Starting and Stopping. Whichever position is chosen, pressure of the lever to the right opens the decompressor, so that one pedals off thus with the roller in the drive position. As the lever is released—normally with the ball of the right thumb—the side of the first finger presses it to the left, opening the throttle. A left-hander would use finger-side for decompressor and thumb for throttle.

To stop, in traffic or elsewhere, temporarily or permanently, the throttle is closed and the decompressor opened. To restart is easy by following the procedure outlined in the previous paragraph.

The "Synchromatic" Power Pak. This aroused much interest at the 1952 Motor Cycle Show, and is a little dearer. On this model there is no decompressor, and instead of the "fingertip" control there is a twist-grip. If this is fitted as normally to the right handlebar it opens the throttle when twisted towards the rider. It could be fitted to the left bar, but in this case the open movement becomes away from the rider.

A second cable leads from the twist-grip to a small single-plate clutch ingeniously incorporated in the main drive shaft. This includes the "synchromatic" mechanism.

THE POWER PAK

Twisting the grip to the right closes the throttle. Continuing the movement causes the clutch to separate, interrupting the drive to the roller. The roller, therefore, "freewheels" upon the tyre. If the throttle is set at the carburettor so that the full twist of the grip to the right does not fully close it, the Power-Pak rider can come to a stop in traffic with the engine running lightly,

Fig. 31. The "Synchromatic" Power Pak

instead of having to stall it each time. For the unmechanical rider in particular this greatly simplifies control.

If one does want to stop the engine there is no difficulty about this. With the cycle stationary and a brake applied, the first twist of the grip to the left causes the clutch to engage and the engine will stall.

As the word "synchromatic" implies, the mechanism incorporates a synchronizing device by which the rider cannot fail to get a perfectly smooth start, provided of course the brakes are released and, preferably, the machine encouraged to move by light pedal strokes. The clutch will not engage abruptly no matter how fast the twist-grip is turned.

As the grip is turned completely to the right the sequence of events is that, first, the throttle is closed, or reduced to tick-over point. Second, the drive and driven parts of the clutch separate so that the mainshaft ceases to be driven. Third, a dogged sleeve splined to this shaft slides out of engagement with corresponding dogs on the roller sleeve.

The sleeve on the mainshaft makes a short lateral movement along its splines, but of course cannot turn independently of the shaft. The roller sleeve is restrained sideways, but it is free to rotate, either independently in "freewheeling" or with the mainshaft when the dogs re-engage. Turning the grip back to the left re-enacts the sequence of events with automatic smoothness, in reverse.

Starting the engine is thus even simpler than when a decompressor is fitted. The rider pedals away and, when a little speed has been gained, twists in the grip to engage the clutch and open the throttle, and the engine will fire. In the free clutch position the roller can be left to turn idly with the tyre, and in fact the synchromatic device eliminates any need to lift the roller away from the tyre.

This is beneficial because it is only when there is movement in the form of slip between roller and tyre that wear can occur through this cause. The grooves remain geared to the tyre. There is also the interesting probability that the free-spinning roller would act as a puncture-preventor in either drive or free position. Nails or flints never cause a puncture at their first impact but only when they are gradually driven through the tyre by repeated impact upon the road. The roller should flick out such intruders before they could penetrate the cover, acting in fact much like the puncture guards fitted by some cyclists across the forks of the machine.

CHAPTER XIX

THE TEAGLE

W. T. Teagle (Machinery) Ltd.
Blackwater, Truro, Cornwall

The Teagle cyclemotor is made by a firm of West Country agricultural engineers, and is basically a "square" (40 × 40 mm., 49 c.c.) two-stroke driving the rear wheel from the carrier position. It is retained by clips attaching it to the saddle tube and rear down-members, and by a stirrup mounting to the rear spindle ends. Three-point rubber insulated suspension is used.

The Power Unit. Cylinder barrel, crankcase, and outrigger-bearing bracket form a single casting, eliminating gaskets throughout these parts. The detachable aluminium cylinder head is heavily finned and has a brass insert to receive the 14 mm. sparking plug, which can thus be removed and replaced indefinitely without damage to the thread.

A Wellworthy liner and piston assembly is used, the liner having a bridged exhaust port. The piston is of the deflector type. The liner is inserted by differential expansion at 750°F., and the piston pin is inserted through the inlet ports. The gas transfer-passage is outside the cylinder liner and the incoming gases enter the head opposite the exhaust port giving unidirectional flow.

The engine lies horizontally with the head to the rear, and there is a shield between it and the tapering three-quarter gallon "petroil" tank, so that in effect the power unit is largely enclosed. Cooling is not dependent upon exposure to the air, as the Bantamag generator, upon the near-side end of the crankshaft, has cooling fins cast upon the flywheel. The engine is in fact blower-cooled, in the makers' own description.

Since cooling is thus positive, it is claimed that a "cool" plug, as distinct from the heat-resistant types usually fitted to two-strokes, can be employed. A cool-running plug has a greater resistance to oiling up than a "hot" one. The makers also state that long periods are possible between successive decarbonizings since there is no tendency to pre-ignition from hot carbon deposits in the head or on the piston crown. Maintenance, in other words, should be considerably reduced.

The tubular exhaust system can be removed and taken apart

by unscrewing two nuts, at the same time exposing the exhaust ports: the point at which it is most essential to keep a two-stroke engine clean. The overhead shield which covers the engine and acts as a cowl to the fan draught is removed with the cylinder head, by removing two studs and four nuts. A tool-kit of five spanners and a screwdriver is supplied with the engine.

FIG. 32. THE TEAGLE

The connecting-rod is drop-forged from R.R. 56 alloy and the bearing bores are burnished. The fabricated steel crankshaft is ground to fine limits and there is the refinement of a centrifugal lubrication system to the crankpin. Oil seals protect all bearings, which should thus be assured of a long life since they do not have to depend upon "petroil" mist.

A Replacement Engine. If, after a considerable mileage major engine reconditioning is required, a replacement engine, less carburettor and flywheel magneto, can be supplied from Teagle agents in exchange at £4. Alternatively the engine can be sent back to the makers for reconditioning at a low price. This ensures accurate work and a better result than the amateur can obtain.

Fuel and Carburation. Carburation is by a needle-less B.E.C. carburettor and petrol to oil strength is 20 to 1. Mixture strength is regulated by a screw behind the main (single) jet which varies the vacuum. A separate starting chamber can be filled to any

Fig. 33. The Teagle as Fitted

desired level, high in cold weather or not used at all in the summer. For very cold weather SAE 10 oil, a very light grade, is recommended, and SAE 20 for other occasions.

A sediment-trapping bowl filter passes the fuel to the carburettor, in the inlet of which there is also a gauze, so that clean fuel should always reach the engine even if it is not strained into the tank. The filler cap of this has an anti-splash device and an oil measure.

The Controls. A toggle lever on the handlebars controls the pressure of the hardened steel drive roller. This is cut with gear teeth which soon become in effect geared to the tyre. Rollers are supplied in $1\frac{5}{8}$ in. or $1\frac{7}{8}$ in. for hilly or level use, and the handlebar toggle varies the pressure to suit wet or dry weather. Owing to its toothed construction the roller should not be lowered on to the moving tyre when starting—one should pedal away with the teeth engaging the tread. The only other extra control is the lever throttle.

The engine is claimed to develop up to $1\frac{1}{2}$ h.p. Equipment, in addition to the tools already mentioned, covers both number-plates, licence-holder, and rear lamp. The Teagle has a year's guarantee.

CHAPTER XX

THE VAP 4

FRANK LAWRENCE MOTOR CYCLES
125 Falcon Road, London, S.W.11

EXTENSIVE experience in the production of small auxiliary motors for cycles lies behind the French VAP 4 cyclemotor. The engine is an "over-square" two-stroke (40 × 38 mm. bore and stroke, 48 c.c. capacity) using a deflector piston and the conventional three-port system. Mounting of the engine is upon the rear-wheel spindle. Final drive is by chain to a large sprocket bolted to the rear-wheel spoke intersections.

Fuel (half a gallon) is carried in a neat wedge-shaped tank on the near-side member of the rear parcels grid. A matching toolbox can be fitted to the off-side. As well as the throttle and decompressor control on the right handlebar there is a friction clutch operated from the left grip. It disconnects the drive at will exactly as in a full-sized motor cycle.

The Fuel Mixture and Performance. At the normally recommended cruising speed of 15–20 m.p.h. the engine revolutions are 3,500 per minute. Peak speed is 5,000 r.p.m. at which the VAP 4 develops 1·2 h.p. (road speed 25 m.p.h.). A "petroil" mixture of 1 part oil to 8 parts petrol is recommended for running-in, after which (300 miles) the strength can be reduced to 1 to 12½.

Weight (engine alone) is 17·6 lb. Aluminium alloy is used for all static engine parts. Crankcase, cylinder barrel, and head are separate, with the barrel sleeved with cast iron. Little and big-end bearings turn on needle rollers with double row balls for each of the mains.

At the front end of the crankcase casting there is an integral projecting platform. Two vertical bolts inset in this carry an oscillating and shock-absorbing arm by which the power unit is secured to the rear-wheel spindle.

Ignition. This is by a rotating-magnet unit mounted within the near-side of the crankcase. It is made by the proprietors of the engine and driven direct from the end of the crankshaft. The 14 mm. sparking plug is also produced by the ABG concern.

Construction. Alternative carburettor equipment is either an ABG of unusual design or a Zenith MKG. The ABG carburettor

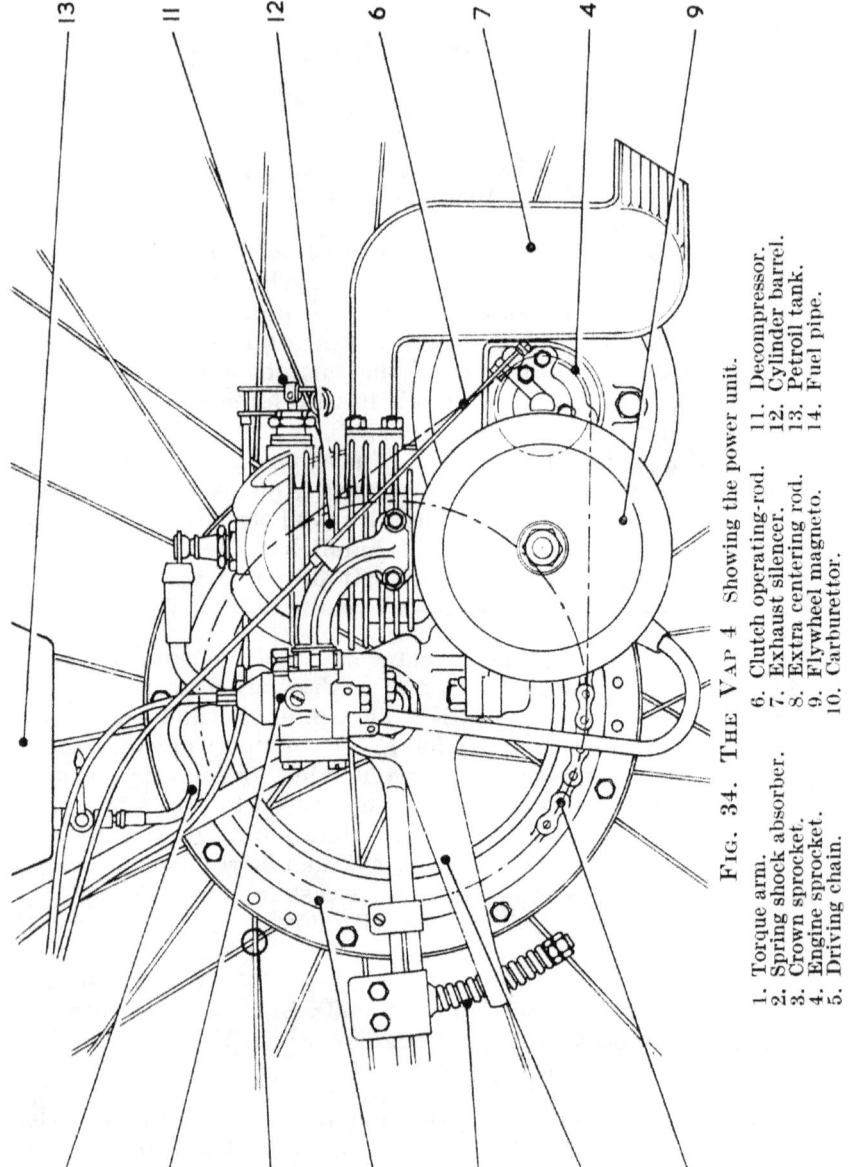

FIG. 34. THE VAP 4 Showing the power unit.

1. Torque arm.
2. Spring shock absorber.
3. Crown sprocket.
4. Engine sprocket.
5. Driving chain.
6. Clutch operating rod.
7. Exhaust silencer.
8. Extra centering rod.
9. Flywheel magneto.
10. Carburettor.
11. Decompressor.
12. Cylinder barrel.
13. Petrol tank.
14. Fuel pipe.

THE VAP 4

is completely enclosed and very compact, with novel features designed to render maintenance as simple as possible for the non-technical user.

There is a snap-on fuel line. This is flexible, attached and detached by pressing on or pulling up at the junction point. Then there is an almost entirely automatic air flap.

This, within the range up to full throttle, is raised and lowered by the throttle cable. The rider can start and warm up the engine without touching the carburettor. Once the engine is warm the rider momentarily opens the throttle fully, an action which lifts the flap right out of the way, where it remains. Before the next time of starting from cold it must be pushed down manually.

Cleaning the Jet. The single jet also acts as one of two bolts retaining the carburettor front in position. Should the jet become obstructed it can be unscrewed with a coin and withdrawn without disturbing any other part or emptying the carburettor. At the end of the jet is a small extension, threaded to fit a cycle pump. It is only the work of a few seconds to screw the jet to the pump and blow out any obstruction.

The final feature is a spring blade at the base of the carburettor. Pushing this down opens a valve at the lowest point of the instrument. Any fine foreign matter passing the two filters accumulates here in a small sump, which is thus emptied and the dirt flushed away without need to take the instrument apart.

The valve can also be used as a quick check that fuel is reaching the carburettor. It is not, however, a flooding device, and in fact the ABG carburettor does not use the conventional type of flooder in which the float is depressed to raise the fuel level above normal.

The float is solid and unpuncturable. Its unusual shape and composition, and fine clearance with the roof of the float chamber, require great care in dismantling. It rises and falls from a hinge at one side.

Of conventional design, the Zenith MKG instrument is of top-feed type. A single jet at the base of the mixing chamber supplies fuel varying with the raising or lowering of a slide by cable control. The cylindrical float is depressed by a tickler to flood for ease in starting, and a swing flap controls admission of air.

The Engine Mounting. The near-side spindle nut is replaced by an extension piece locked in position by a tab washer between it and the frame. The extension has a cylindrical bearing, and over this slides an eccentric collar. This is retained within its housing in the engine mounting arm by a pinch bolt.

When the collar and engine arm are in position they are retained endwise by a dome nut and washer assembly which allows the arm rotational freedom. The collar is made eccentric to permit adjustment to the pedalling chain.

A forward extension of the arm is held between two springs upon a curved rod secured by a clip and bolts to the lower frame-member. The end of the rod is threaded to take two nuts locked against each other. The arm has thus a small radial movement limited by the restraint of the springs, which provide the shock-absorption effect.

Below the collar bearing, a platform engages the corresponding platform projecting from the forward edge of the engine crankcase. The two are bolted together, the engine arm platform being slotted for adjustment during fitting. The whole engine can thus turn slightly against the springs in either direction, so that the torque is absorbed by the springs. Provision is made for lubricating the collar.

The Sprocket Drive. As already indicated the crown sprocket is bolted to the spokes at the near-side of the wheel. Either British cycles, with 40-spoke wheels, or French and continental cycles generally, with 36 spokes, can be accommodated by varying the mounting points.

The crown sprocket itself, integral with the mounting ring, has 54 teeth. The driving sprocket has 15 teeth. In cases where the machine is to be used in very hilly country a 12-tooth driving sprocket can be supplied. With the 54 to 15 ratio a 63-link driving chain is fitted. The lower gear (54 to 12) takes a chain of 62 links, and there is the usual type of removable link in the chain.

A countershaft carries the driving sprocket. Splined and locked upon this is the inner, fabric-faced component of a cone clutch. At the far end of the countershaft the inner element of the clutch slides upon splines and is forced outwards by a powerful internal coil spring.

Upon the end of the countershaft a rack-and-pinion device operated by the left handlebar lever pushes the clutch cone inwards and so disengages the drive. When the lever is released the cone moves outwards and its friction surface presses upon the inner face of the outer component. This constitutes a gear ring, the helical gear on its outer surface being in permanent mesh with a smaller pinion on the inner end of the crankshaft.

The drive therefore passes through this small pinion, which has 15 or 18 teeth according to the type of use of the machine. It continues through the larger helical-geared pinion, which has 68 or 73 teeth, and in this way undergoes a reduction rather greater than 4 to 1. The motor or driving sprocket receives the geared-down drive and transmits it through the driving chain to the crown

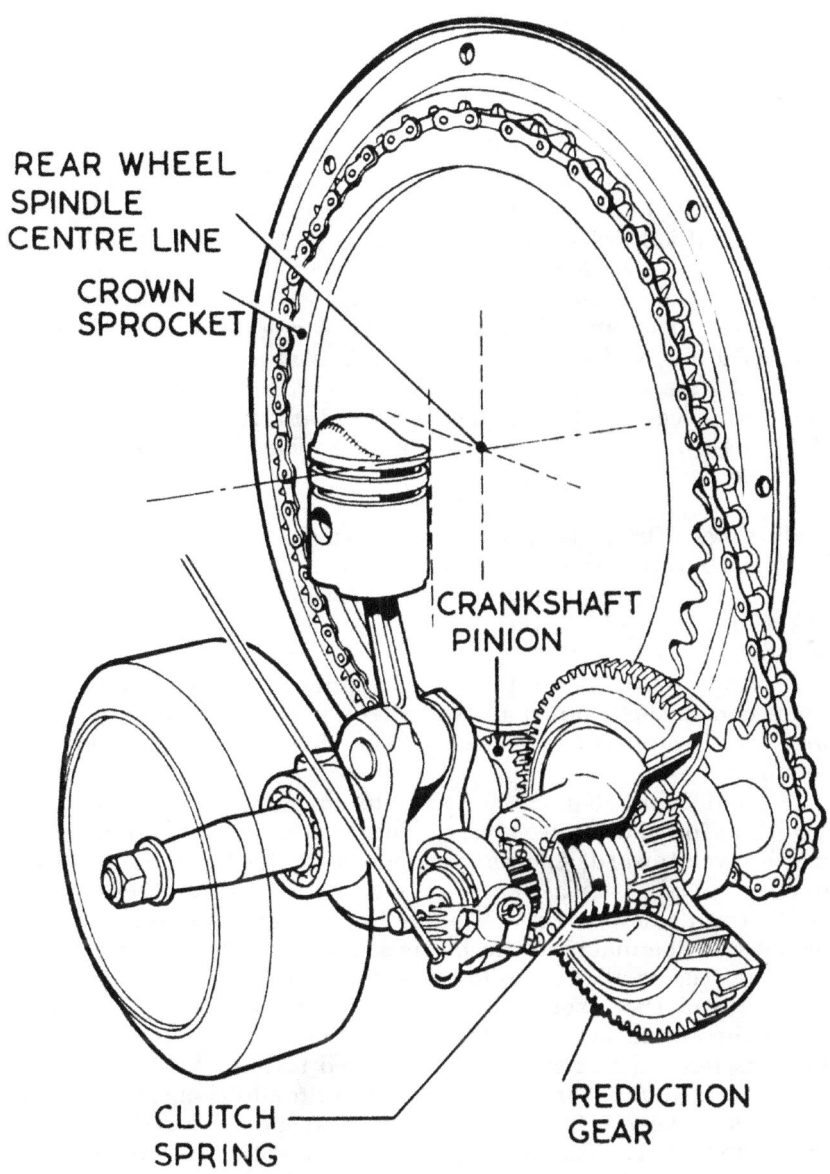

Fig. 35. The Vap 4
Simplified diagram showing the engine in relation to the cycle rear-wheel.

sprocket. The first reduction was, say, 4 to 1 and that through the two pinions is about $3\frac{1}{2}$ to 1. Total reduction is thus something approaching 15 to 1.

After 400 miles. The reduction gear runs in oil and the makers emphasize that the level should be checked every 400 miles. A small plug is unscrewed and the level adjusted with an oil gun so that the oil is level with the lower part of the screw thread. The plug is found between the bottom of the silencer and the clutch operating rack-and-pinion mechanism.

As previously mentioned, the VAP-4 engine, especially when new, is designed to take an oil-petrol mixture containing rather more oil than usual. After checking the reduction-gear level it is therefore necessary to see that the fuel tank is filled with a blend of 1 part oil to 8 parts petrol (this is replaced by 1 to $12\frac{1}{2}$ after covering the first 300 miles).

Starting. First, the fuel tap is turned on. With the Zenith MKG carburettor the tickler is depressed while the rider carefully watches for the first ooze of fuel. As soon as this is sighted the tickler is released, and the choke flap is turned to the closed position.

With the ABG carburettor, which cannot be flooded, the spring blade can be held down until "petroil" is seen to emerge. The only other check is to ensure that the choke slide is pushed right down.

The left handlebar carries the clutch control, with a locking trigger as on most autocycles. The first part of the movement of the lever towards the handlebar disengages the clutch. If the lever is pulled as far as it will go a cam beneath the trigger locks the lever in this position. The engine is then completely disconnected and the machine can be ridden like an ordinary bicycle.

If the trigger above the lever is depressed, the internal cam is released and the lever returns to the fully outward position (in which the clutch is engaged). To start the machine the clutch is fully disengaged and the lever is allowed to lock.

The right handlebar has two controls (in addition, of course, to the brake lever). One, moving vertically and pressed down for operation, works the decompressor. The other is the throttle lever, opening with a movement towards the rider.

After four or five revolutions of the pedals the decompressor is pushed down at the same time that the clutch is released. Almost immediately the throttle is opened a little and the decompressor released. The engine should start at once.

CHAPTER XXI

THE VELOSOLEX

SOLEX (CYCLES) LTD.
223-231 Marylebone Rd., London, N.W.1

FRENCH in origin, the VeloSoleX is sold as a complete cycle of stout and in some ways unusual construction. It is fitted with a simple two-stroke engine driving the front wheel through a roller. The engine is on a hinged bracket and a trigger locking device retains it when in the "off" position.

The Power Unit. The engine is a three-port two-stroke of 45 c.c. (38 × 40 mm. bore and stroke) developing 0·4 h.p. at 2,000 revs. For lubrication 1 part oil is mixed with 16 parts petrol—best done, as usual, in a separate container. A consumption of 300 m.p.g. is claimed at the cruising speed of 16 m.p.h., and the weight of the entire bicycle is 60 lb.

A neat and symmetrical appearance is given to the engine by the Solex flywheel-magneto on the near-side, in its dome-shaped casing, balanced at the off-side by a fuel tank of exactly the same dimensions. The front registration marks are conveniently painted on the flat outer surface of these two units, repeated at each side as is the case with motor cycles when a single front-facing plate is not used.

Carburation. The fuel tank holds 1¾ pints (one litre) giving a range of 60 miles. An interesting point of the VeloSoleX is that it lacks a fuel tap, and indeed could not be fitted with one since the level of the fuel is lower than its point of entry into the engine. A membrane fuel pump draws it up and lifts it into the carburettor, whence an overflow pipe returns any surplus to the tank.

The pump is without moving parts and is entirely actuated by the varying pressure within the crankcase. As soon as the engine starts to turn the crankcase pressure falls below that of the outer atmosphere, which is in communication with the membrane. This therefore moves inwards and draws "petroil" from the tank to fill the pump. Once the fuel passes into the carburettor and so into the crankcase, the low pressure here rises with the descent of the piston. The membrane is now distended in the reverse direction and the whole pumpful of fuel is blown up into the carburettor.

This instrument, a Solex, deviates from the conventional order.

There is neither float nor float chamber, nor is there a needle valve. A single jet atomizes the rising fuel, which passes down a short swan-neck induction pipe to the inlet port in the upper part of the crankcase. Apart from the throttle, the only control for the

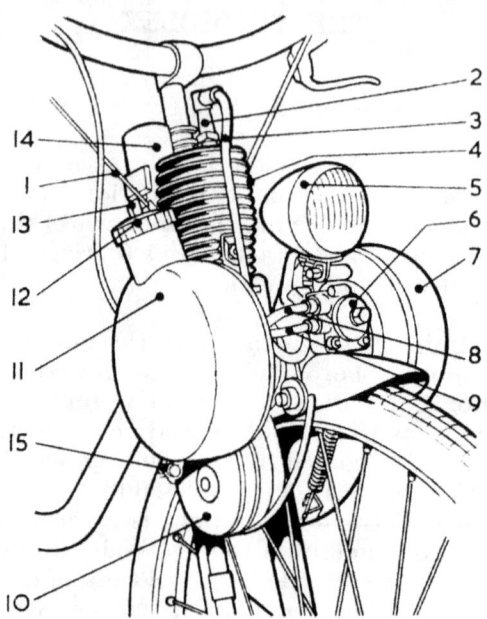

Fig. 36. The VeloSoleX

1. Throttle control.
2. Sparking plug.
3. H.T. cable.
4. Cylinder head.
5. Headlamp.
6. Petroil pump.
7. Flywheel magneto.
8, 9. Fuel pipes, pump to carburettor, and tank pump.
10. Exhaust silencer.
11. Petroil tank.
12. Tank filler-cap/oil measure.
13. Carburettor.
14. Air intake silencer.
15. "Petroil" tank drain plug.

rider is the choke which closes off the air for starting in cold weather.

The Lighting. Coils, within the flywheel magneto, supply current as long as the engine is running, to a 6-volt 1-amp. headlamp which can be mounted centrally on the forepart of the crankcase, or on a clip attached to the steering column. The coils also operate a 6-volt 0·04-amp. rear light. For parking there is a 3·5-volt bulb also within the headlight running off a dry battery in the lamp case.

Starting. Throttle control has been simplified as much as possible for the non-mechanical user. A hinged thumb lever is

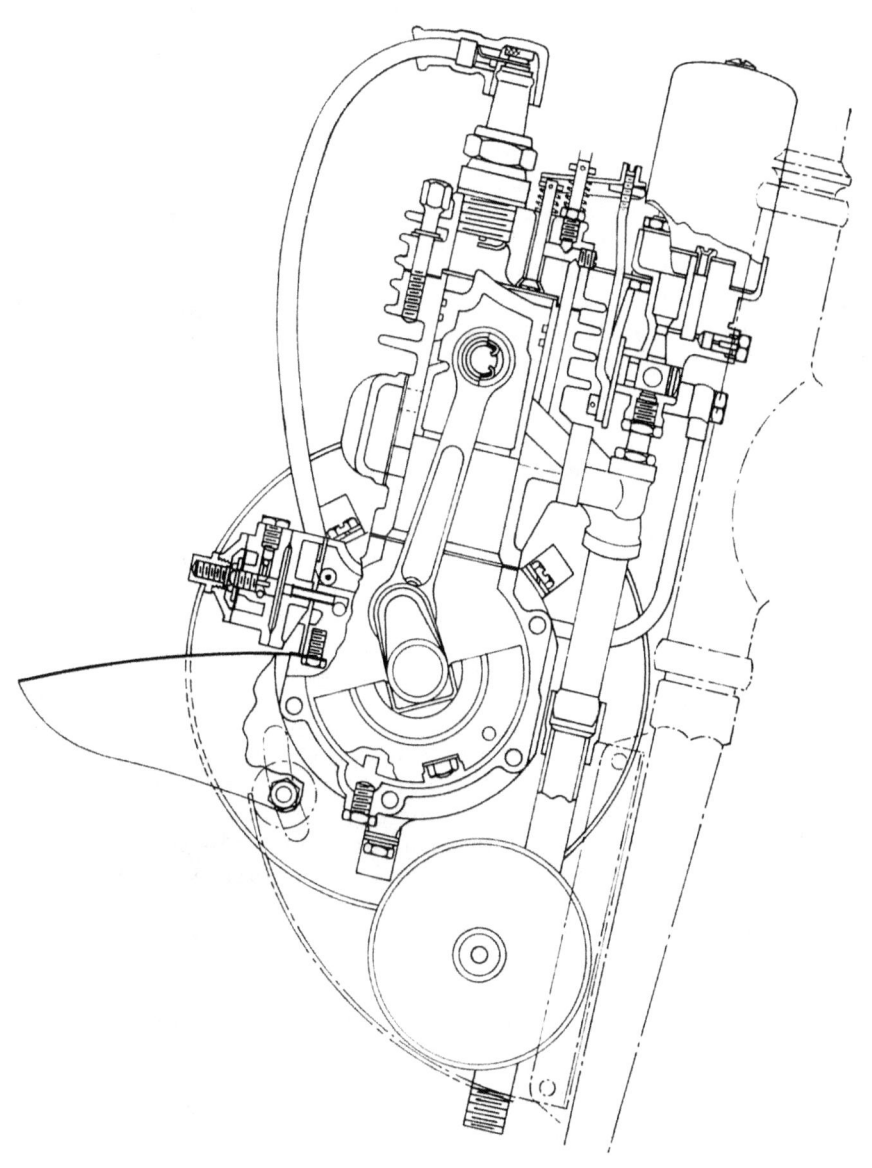

Fig. 37. The VeloSoleX Engine in Cross-section

fitted just inside the left handlebar grip. Pressing this against the bar closes the throttle and opens the decompressor so that the cycle, with the roller on the tyre, can be pedalled away for starting. The lever is spring-loaded so that when, after a few turns of the pedals, the rider releases it, the decompressor is closed and the throttle opened automatically to the full.

As the makers emphasize, the lever is only moved when starting, and thereafter to decrease speed or to stop. When running normally on the road the lever is left alone. To slow or stop, the rider pushes it against the bar and applies the brakes. It is of course important to observe this drill when stopping, first to press the lever against the bar, which opens the decompressor and brings the braking effect of the engine into play, and then to apply the brakes.

Starting from Cold. The choke adds very little even to the non-mechanical driver's responsibilities. In starting from cold a lever at the base of the carburettor, painted red to distinguish it, is moved over to the left. After a few yards of running, when the engine begins to warm, this red lever should be moved back to the previous position. There is no need to dismount to do this. Both operations can be performed in motion from the saddle and are soon sufficiently familiar to be done without looking down.

Engaging the Drive. This is easy and could be done from the saddle, though it is not a good idea to get into the habit of doing so. A trigger or locking nut protrudes from the lower rear part of the magneto casing, at the near side. On lifting this up the engine can be rocked back and forth by grasping the top of the carburettor. Pushing the engine forward brings the carborundum-faced roller beneath the crankcase into contact with the front tyre. To lift the roller and free the drive so that the machine can be ridden like an ordinary cycle, it is not necessary to touch the locking nut, but only to curl the fingers round the top of the carburettor with the thumb as a lever round the steering post. The engine can then be pulled back until it locks with a click in the "off" position (it does not lock in this way when taking up the "drive" position).

The engine is mounted upon a hinged sub-frame with two rubber bushes between the hinge pin and its bearing. When swung into the drive position the engine is restrained there by two coil springs. The combined effect of these springs and the rubber mounting is to give a shock-absorbing effect between the drive roller and the tyre.

The Exhaust and Silencer. Exhaust gases are led from the engine into a disc-shaped silencer or expansion chamber beneath the "petroil" tank at the off-side of the machine. From the silencer a long pipe of small diameter goes down to a point at the bottom of the front mudguard where there is the least likelihood of oily fumes being blown back on to the rider's clothing.

The Cycle Frame. Since the engine and cycle are built together, reference to the frame brings out interesting points. The whole machine has a distinctly more sturdy appearance than an ordinary pedal cycle. The makers maintain that the extra stresses imposed upon a cycle by an auxiliary engine must be offset by more robust construction.

Only one model is built, and it has an open swan-neck frame of thick and rigid build. This frame is assembled from four separate groups: main tube, main fork assembly, upper rear fork assembly, and lower rear forks. All fork blades are channel pressings. No cross-bar is necessary, and one model serves for a man or a woman.

The Brakes. Caliper brakes with inverted levers are fitted. Cables to the rear wheel, including lighting wires, pass through the swan-neck frame. Spindle and bottom-bracket bearings are sealed in grease at the factory and need no attention. Pedals are completely rubber covered. Chain guard, rear carrier, metal toolbox with full kit, and a large water-repellent saddle are supplied.

The Tyres. Semi-balloon tyres ($1\frac{3}{4} \times 1\frac{1}{2}$ in.) help riding comfort. It is claimed that if the tyres—which have a tread designed for the machine—are kept inflated hard there is no more wear on the front tyre than on the rear. Normal front tyre wear averages about 4,000 miles.

Trouble-free Running. The rider of a VeloSoleX power-assisted cycle desires, above all things, trouble-free running. This, the makers state, can be had with little effort if attention is paid to a small number of seemingly insignificant points. For example, one of the commonest causes of erratic running in small two-stroke engines is carelessness with the "petroil" mixture. A grade of lubricating oil is recommended by each maker and instructions are given for its mixture with petrol in the correct proportions.

Mixing the Fuel. Make up the "petroil" mixture in a clean separate container and shake it well up before transferring it to the tank of the machine. Apart from the fact that most garages dislike supplying small odd quantities of petrol to cyclemotor owners, a proper mixture will not result from pouring petrol into the tank, adding so many measures of oil, and then shaking the machine in the pious hope that a true "petroil" mixture will result. More probably undissolved lubricating oil will fill all the pipes and passages, forcing the owner to take everything to pieces, perhaps by the roadside.

When the separate mixture has been made up, pour it into the tank through a proper petrol funnel having a fine-mesh gauze strainer incorporated in its neck. Fluff, dirt, and water will be trapped here instead of entering the tank and later clogging filters and jets.

Always use the grade of oil specified by the makers. The VeloSoleX engine is designed to operate on an oil of SAE 10 specification. This is a light oil, and its use enables mileages of the order of 2,000 and more to be covered before decarbonization becomes necessary. If heavier oils are used, SAE 20 or 30 viscosity say, carbon will form more rapidly. The SAE specification method is now used and understood by all garages as a convenient and unmistakable indication of the "body" of oils. Most branded oils now publish their SAE specification, the "body" being heavier with the larger numbers.

Carbon formation is much more important in a small engine than a large one. It causes a rapid falling off in power, particularly, as is emphasized elsewhere in this book, when it occurs in the exhaust system.

The Sparking Plug. This is another item to which regular attention should be given. That fitted to the engine by the makers is the one proved by test to be most suitable. Experiment with other types often causes erratic operation of the power unit. The plug should be cleaned, and the gap at the points reset, regularly every few hundred miles instead of waiting for misfiring. Easy starting and good performance will be the reward.

Then if the rider adopts a good technique the behaviour of the machine will be greatly improved. The VeloSoleX is like other small-engined makes in that it is a power-assisted cycle—not a powered cycle. The machine is there to help, not to do all the work all the time. The power output of the motor will take the rider along the road, on the level, and up any average gradient without pedalling. But, on a steep hill the wise rider pedals early and helps the engine. If the little unit is allowed to slog itself to a standstill, or if pedal help is given too late, heavy strain is thrown on the bearings and they will wear out prematurely. By helping the engine whenever it cannot run lightly and easily, overhauls and expense can be long postponed.

Decarbonizing. Some owners like to undertake simple maintenance work themselves. The VeloSoleX engine is straightforward to maintain if certain points are remembered. Decarbonizing is a job that numerous users prefer to perform for themselves and there is no reason why this should not be done quite successfully.

As emphasized in the earlier chapter "Looking After Your Cyclemotor," cleanliness and freedom from carbon in the exhaust system is quite as important as removing carbon from the cylinder head and piston crown: frequently more so. The VeloSoleX is no exception. Therefore when the cylinder head has been removed and the piston cleaned, turn the engine by hand until the piston is at its lowest point in the barrel. This exposes the exhaust port in the cylinder wall. Examine this port. There is bound to be some formation of carbon; no matter how slight, it should be removed. A small blunt screwdriver can be used here if it is particularly obstinate, but a sharpened slip of oak cannot cause scratches.

Considerable carbon deposits round the port indicate that the pipe to the silencer will also be partly choked. Clean out this pipe and do not forget the silencer itself. The VeloSoleX silencer can be dismantled, which makes cleaning the inside much easier. Many a proud amateur who polishes up his piston and cylinder head cannot understand why the machine does not go better. This is what happens if he forgets the exhaust system, back-pressure in which ruins the engine's performance.

In reassembling after decarbonizing renew all gaskets and washers. It is false economy to replace old ones. No jointing compound should be used, but gaskets can be lightly smeared with clean grease before they are pressed into position.

Cleaning. The VeloSoleX makers also emphasize the importance of a clean engine. Road dust, oil, and mud on the outside of the power unit, or on the cycle, render it impossible to see when nuts and bolts start to work loose or when joints and gaskets leak. Dirt on the outside of the engine also has a remarkable habit of finding its own way inside. Work on a dirty engine takes twice as long because it must be cleaned down before adjustments can be made. On all scores, therefore, keep the whole machine, and especially the engine, as clean as it is when new.

CHAPTER XXII

THE VINCENT "FIREFLY"

VINCENT ENGINEERS (STEVENAGE) LTD.
Stevenage, Herts.

THE two-stroke Vincent "Firefly" is mounted below the bottom bracket and drives the rear tyre of the cycle through a cast-iron roller of $3\frac{1}{4}$ in. diameter which has a tread of deep transverse ribs. With bore and stroke 38 × 42 mm. and capacity 48 c.c., the engine is of the deflectorless piston type—the piston is noticeably domed—developing nearly one horse power at 3,800 r.p.m.

The Fuel. A "petroil" mixture of 1 part oil to 20 of petrol is fed through a small Amal carburettor. When running steadily with a properly matured engine at speeds up to 25 m.p.h. the makers state that a fuel consumption of up to 180 m.p.g. may be expected.

The Power Unit. The weight of the engine is 18 lb. All-up, including mountings of a five-eighths gallon "petroil" tank and controls, it weighs under 24 lb. Width is dimensioned to give clearance between the pedal cranks, and in case of any difficulty a spindle extension can be fitted to the bottom bracket giving about an extra inch of clearance. The engine rides 4 in. from the ground.

Cylinder head and split crankcase are in light alloy, the barrel being cast iron. The exceptionally long Lo-Ex piston, fitted with two pegged rings, is cut away in the skirt to prevent the transfer port being masked too long. Four long-nutted studs hold the head and barrel to the crankcase. Conventional inlet, transfer, and exhaust porting is used, with the transfer angled to prevent contamination.

The Engine Mounting. This is effected at three points. There is first a stout bracket clipped to the bottom of the front down tube. Two plates, provided with three-point adjustments, suspend the engine from immediately behind the induction stub of the forward-mounted carburettor. This mounting provides a hinge. There is then a sliding fitment attaching extensions in the crankcase to the lower rear-fork tubes behind the bottom bracket. Finally a stay runs from the rear of the crankcase to an extension below the rear spindle at the near side.

THE VINCENT "FIREFLY" 103

This steady stay incorporates a toggle mechanism. A cable midway along the stay runs vertically up and along the frame to a control on the left handlebar.

This has the effect of a clutch lever. Drawing the lever towards the handlebar slides the unit rearward and so the roller against the tyre. The lever locks in the compressed position by a cam which can be released by the forefinger. Adjustments to the

FIG. 38. THE VINCENT FIREFLY (NEARSIDE VIEW)

steady stay and the bottom bracket fitment complete the means by which the "Firefly" can be adapted to any bicycle.

The Miller Electrical System. This includes an a.c. generator designed for the engine. This is driven at half-crankshaft speed by an enclosed gear drive at the near side of the unit which also transmits power to the large ribbed roller. The generator energizes an ignition coil housed in a recess at the bottom of the fuel tank clipped to the front down-tube.

At the opposite or off-side end of the crankshaft is the contact-breaker. The end of the crankshaft is hollow and formed with an internal cam. Upon this the lobe of the contact-breaker rides and is lifted during each revolution of the shaft.

The fixed point is mounted upon a back plate secured by three screws. One of these is eccentric so that while at the factory the engine is receiving its bench test the timing can be fine-set as the engine runs, to give the best power output. The moving point

FIG. 39. THE VINCENT FIREFLY (OFFSIDE VIEW)

also has the refinement of an eccentric screw mounting enabling the gap to be set with great precision.

Lighting coils are fitted in the generator. They will give current for head and tail lights at 10–12 m.p.h. and can also operate a lightweight electric horn.

The generator assembly is masked by a chrome cover directly underneath the pedalling chainwheel. A spring clip holds the cover. If the pedalling chain is enclosed in a gear case it may be necessary to mount the engine somewhat farther to the near side so as to allow enough clearance between the gear case and the generator cover plate. In this case the spindle extension already mentioned is fitted to the near-side bottom bracket spindle. This

THE VINCENT "FIREFLY"

enables the pedal crank to clear the light alloy case bearing the maker's name which encloses the reduction gear.

Rubber bonds the shell of the cast-iron driving roller to its steel shaft and gives a considerable resilience to the drive. The shaft is supported at each end by a journal bearing.

Having in mind that impaction of the silencer is a frequent trouble with two-strokes, the makers of the "Firefly" have provided a silencer which is easily dismantled. It is of flattened box shape fitted direct to the exhaust port on the under-side of the cylinder barrel. Two bolts, passing through laterally, can be withdrawn and the silencer then comes into three parts.

A decompressor is fitted, controlled by outward movement of the throttle lever. The rider is recommended always to pedal away with the roller engaged and the decompressor open. After four turns of the pedals the throttle lever is moved inwards and to the left, closing the decompressor and opening the throttle, when the engine will fire at once.

Overhaul and Servicing. These have been simplified by making the "Firefly" easy to dismantle, even to splitting the flywheels. All main and countershaft bearings are ball journal of the same size and the assemblies are largely interchangeable. The small end is a phosphor-bronze bush with a floating gudgeon-pin. The big end has caged roller bearings.

The air intake of the carburettor faces forward but air is drawn in at the back of the choke cowl and this incorporates a wire-wool cleaner. The compression ratio, 5 to 1, enables non-premium fuel to be used. The choke is controlled by a vertical lever projecting from the cowl.

INDEX

ABG Magneto and carburettor, 89
Acceleration, poor, 23
Accidents, 5
Air leaks, 20
Alfa forks, 79
Amal carburettor, 16, 30, 73, 82, 102
Auto-Minor (ABJ), 28

"Bantamag" magneto, 24, 82, 85
B.E.C. carburettor, 87
Belt drive, 41, 69
Berini, 32
Blower cooling, 85
Bottom feed carburettor, 17
Brakes, 6, 71
  internal expanding, 38
Britax cycle, 53
B.S.A. "Winged Wheel," 37

Carborundum roller, 29, 32, 62, 72
Carburettor—
  ABG, 89
  Amal, 102
  B.E.C., 87
  Dellorto, 57, 76
  Solex, 95
Caustic soda, 11
Centrifugal clutch, 71
Certificate of Insurance, 1, 3
Chain drive, 89
Choke, 41
Claim form, 5
Clutch—
  adjustment, 48
  drive, 37, 45, 50, 82, 89, 92
Compression—
  ignition, 58
  ratio, 51, 60
Contact breaker, 25
Crankcase drain screw, 40
"Cucciolo," 50
Cut-away, throttle, 23
Cyclaid, 41
Cycle, checking, 6

Cyclemaster, 45
Cyclometer, 9

Decarbonizing, 49, 61, 67, 74, 78, 100
Decompressor, 15, 28, 57, 65, 82, 94, 98, 105
Deflector piston, 69, 73, 80, 89
Dellorto carburettor, 57, 76
Diesel engine, 58
Driving—
  licence, 4
  test, 4
DTD alloy, 28
Ducati "Cucciolo," 50
Dunlop cover, 37, 80

Eadie coaster free-wheel, 38
Exhaust system, 10, 74

Filters, 10
Float chamber, 18
Flooding, 17, 23
Flywheel, 26
Forks, spring, 56, 79
Four-stroke, 50
Four-stroking, 44
Fuel, mixing, 9, 99

Gap, points, 14, 31, 40, 54, 67, 77, 100, 104
Gear—
  drive, 37, 77, 92
  reduction, 92, 94
Generator, Miller, 28, 103
Graphited compound, 9
Grease, high melting point, 26

Hesitation, 23
High melting point grease, 26
Highway Code, 4
Horn, 2

Insurance, 2
Itom, 56

Jet, cleaning, 91

106

LICENCE—
    annual, 5
    disc, 2
    driving, 4
    road fund, 1
Lighting coils, 28, 53, 96, 104
"L" plates, 4
Logbook, 1
Lohmann, 58

MAGNETO—
    ABG, 89
    "Bantamag," 24, 82, 85
    Miller, 28, 31, 67
    points, 13, 40
    Solex, 95
Main jet, 20
"Mercury" bicycle, 45
Miller generator, 28, 31, 103
Mini-Motor, 62
Mixture strength, 10
Mobylette, 69
Mocyc, 72
Mosquito, 75

NEEDLE—
    jet carburettor, 47
    position, 20
    seating, 17
Needle-less carburettor, 21
Number plates, 1

OIL seals, 68, 86
"Over-square" engine, 28, 32, 37, 41, 45, 89

PERLITIC cast iron, 76
Pilot jet, 21
Pinking, 61
Piston seizure, 10
Plugs, hot and cool, 85
Policy, insurance, 3
Polishing slip for points, 26
Power Pak, 80
Pre-selector gear, 50
Provisional—
    cover, 3
    licence, 4
Pull-rod valves, 50
Punctures, 49

REDUCTION gear, 44, 59, 75, 76, 94
Registration, 1

Replacement engine, 86
Rich mixture, 15, 19
Riding position, 7
Roller drive, 29, 32, 56, 60, 62, 73, 75, 80, 87, 95, 102
Rotary valve, 32, 45, 46
Running-in, 9, 39, 73

SCHRADER valve, 40
Seizure, piston, 10
Shock-absorber mounting, 92
Slip-sprocket, 53
Solex carburettor, 95
Spark gap, small and large, 14, 26
Sparking plug, 11
    points, 10, 12
Speed, 8
Speedometer, 9
Spitting back, 20
Spring forks, 56, 79
Sprocket drive, 92
"Square" engine, 45, 85
Starting, 7, 35, 39, 44, 47, 53, 60, 65, 73, 77, 82, 84, 94, 96, 98
Strangler (or choke), 17
Synchromatic Power Pak, 81, 82

TAPPET adjustment, 54
Teagle, 85
Test, driving, 4
Third party fire and theft, 2
Throttle faults, 19
Top feed carburettor, 18
"Tourist" Itom, 57
Trojan-Dellorto carburettor, 66
Troubles, tracing, 14, 26
Tuning, 20
Twist-grip, 42, 60, 82
Tyre pressure, 40
Tyres, 7

VAP 4, 89
VeloSoleX, 95
Vincent "Firefly," 102

WEAK mixture, 19
Weber-Cucciolo carburettor, 53, 55
Wellworthy liner and piston, 73, 85
"Whiskering" of plug points, 12, 15

ZENITH MKG carburettor, 89

VELOCEPRESS MANUALS - MOTORCYCLE

1930'S BRITISH MOTORCYCLE CARBS & ELEC COMPONENTS (BOOK OF)
1930'S BRITISH MOTORCYCLE ENGINES (OVERHAUL & MAINTENANCE)
1930'S BRITISH MOTORCYCLE GEARBOXES & CLUTCHES (BOOK OF)
AJS 1932-1948 SINGLES & TWINS 250cc THRU 1000cc (BOOK OF)
AJS 1945-1960 SINGLES 350cc & 500cc MODELS 16 & 18 (BOOK OF)
AJS 1955-1965 SINGLES 350cc & 500cc (BOOK OF)
ARIEL 1932-1939 PREWAR MODELS (BOOK OF)
ARIEL 1933-1951 (WORKSHOP MANUAL)
ARIEL 1939-1960 4 STROKE SINGLES (BOOK OF)
ARIEL 1958-1964 LEADER & ARROW (BOOK OF)
BMW R26 R27 (1956-1967) FACTORY WORKSHOP MANUAL
BMW R50 R50S R60 R69S (1955-1969) FACTORY WORKSHOP MANUAL
BRIDGESTONE 90 SERIES FACTORY WSM & PARTS CATALOGUE
BRIDGESTONE 175 SERIES FACTORY WSM & PARTS CATALOGUE
BSA BANTAM ALL MODELS FROM 1948 ONWARDS (BOOK OF)
BSA SINGLES & V-TWINS UP TO 1927 (BOOK OF)
BSA SINGLES & V-TWINS UP TO 1935 (BOOK OF)
BSA SINGLES & V-TWINS 1936-1939 (BOOK OF)
BSA SINGLES & V-TWINS 1936-1952 (BOOK OF)
BSA OHV & SV SINGLES 250-600cc 1945-1954 (BOOK OF)
BSA OHV & SV SINGLES 250cc 1954-1970 (BOOK OF)
BSA OHV SINGLES 350 & 500cc 1955-1967 (BOOK OF)
BSA TWINS 1948-1962 (BOOK OF)
BSA TWINS 1962-1969 (SECOND BOOK OF)
CYCLEMOTOR (BOOK OF)
DOUGLAS 1929-1939 PREWAR ALL MODELS (BOOK OF)
DOUGLAS 1948-1957 POSTWAR ALL MODELS FACTORY SHOP MANUAL
DUCATI 160cc, 250cc & 350cc OHC MODELS FACTORY SHOP MANUAL
HONDA 50 ALL MODELS UP TO 1970 INC MONKEY & TRAIL (BOOK OF)
HONDA 90 ALL MODELS UP TO 1966 (BOOK OF)
HONDA 125-150cc TWINS C/CS/CB/CA FACTORY WORKSHOP MANUAL
HONDA 250-305 TWINS C/CS/CB FACTORY WORKSHOP MANUAL
HONDA C100 SUPER CUB FACTORY WORKSHOP MANUAL
HONDA C110 SPORT CUB 1962-1969 FACTORY WORKSHOP MANUAL
HONDA TWINS & SINGLES 50cc THRU 305cc 1960-1966 (BOOK OF)
HONDA TWINS ALL MODELS 125cc THRU 450cc UP TO 1968 (BOOK OF)
J.A.P. ENGINES 1927-1952 & MOTORCYCLES 1934-1952 (BOOK OF)
LAMBRETTA 1947-1957 ALL 125 & 150cc MODELS (BOOK OF)
LAMBRETTA 1957-1970 LI & TV MODELS (SECOND BOOK OF)
MATCHLESS 1931-1939 ALL MODELS 250cc THRU 990cc (BOOK OF)
MATCHLESS 1945-1956 350 & 500cc SINGLES (BOOK OF)
MATCHLESS 1955-1966 350 & 500cc SINGLES (BOOK OF)
NEW IMPERIAL ALL SV & OHV FROM 1935 ONWARDS (BOOK OF)
NORTON 1932-1939 PREWAR MODELS (BOOK OF)
NORTON 1932-1947 (BOOK OF)
NORTON 1938-1956 (BOOK OF)
NORTON 1955-1963 MODELS 19, 50 & ES2 (BOOK OF)
NORTON 1955-1965 DOMINATOR TWINS (BOOK OF)
NORTON 1957-1970 TWINS FACTORY WORKSHOP MANUAL
NSU PRIMA 1956-1964 ALL MODELS (BOOK OF)
NSU QUICKLY 1953-1963 ALL MODELS (BOOK OF)
PANTHER 1932-1958 LIGHTWEIGHT MODELS 250 & 350cc (BOOK OF)
PANTHER 1938-1966 HEAVYWEIGHT MODELS 600 & 650cc (BOOK OF)
RALEIGH MOPEDS 1960-1969 (BOOK OF)
RALEIGH MOTORCYCLES 1919-1933 (BOOK OF)
ROYAL ENFIELD 1934-1946 SINGLES & V TWINS (BOOK OF)
ROYAL ENFIELD 1937-1953 SINGLES & V TWINS (BOOK OF)
ROYAL ENFIELD 1946-1962 SINGLES (BOOK OF)
ROYAL ENFIELD 1958-1966 250cc & 350cc SINGLES (SECOND BOOK OF)
ROYAL ENFIELD 736cc INTERCEPTOR FACTORY WORKSHOP MANUAL
RUDGE 1933-1939 (BOOK OF)
SUNBEAM 1928-1939 (BOOK OF)
SUNBEAM 1946-1957 S7 & S8 (BOOK OF)
SUZUKI 50cc & 80cc UP TO 1966 (BOOK OF)
SUZUKI T10 1963-1967 FACTORY WORKSHOP MANUAL
SUZUKI T20 & T200 1965-1969 FACTORY WORKSHOP MANUAL
TRIUMPH 1935-1939 PREWAR MODELS (BOOK OF)
TRIUMPH 1935-1949 (BOOK OF)
TRIUMPH 1937-1951 (WORKSHOP MANUAL)
TRIUMPH 1945-1955 FACTORY WORKSHOP MANUAL
TRIUMPH 1945-1958 TWINS (BOOK OF)
TRIUMPH 1956-1969 TWINS (BOOK OF)
VELOCETTE 1925-1970 ALL SINGLES & TWINS (BOOK OF)
VESPA 1951-1961 (BOOK OF)
VESPA 1955-1963 125 & 150cc & GS MODELS (SECOND BOOK OF)
VESPA 1955-1968 GS & SS (BOOK OF)
VESPA 1963-1972 90, 125 & 150cc (THIRD BOOK OF)
VILLIERS ENGINE UP TO 1959 INC. 3 WHEELERS (BOOK OF)
VILLIERS ENGINE UP TO 1969 (BOOK OF)
VINCENT 1935-1955 (WORKSHOP MANUAL)

VELOCEPRESS TECHNICAL BOOKS – MOTORCYCLE

CATALOG OF BRITISH MOTORCYCLES (1951 MODELS)
INDIAN PONYBIKE, BOY RACER & PAPOOSE ILL PARTS LIST & SALES LIT
MOTORCYCLE ENGINEERING (P.E. Irving)
SPEED AND HOW TO OBTAIN IT (Motor Cycle Magazine UK)
TUNING FOR SPEED (P.E. Irving)

VELOCEPRESS MANUALS - THREE WHEELER'S

BSA THREE WHEELER (BOOK OF)
VINTAGE MORGAN THREE WHEELER (BOOK OF)

VELOCEPRESS MANUALS - AUTOMOBILE

AUSTIN-HEALEY 6-CYLINDER WORKSHOP MANUAL
AUSTIN-HEALEY SPRITE & MG MIDGET WORKSHOP MANUAL 1958-1971
BMW 600 LIMOUSINE FACTORY WORKSHOP MANUAL
BMW 600 LIMOUSINE OWNERS HAND BOOK & SERVICE MANUAL
BMW 2000 & 2002 1966-1976 WORKSHOP MANUAL
BMW ISETTA FACTORY WORKSHOP MANUAL
CORVAIR 1960-1969 WORKSHOP MANUAL
CORVETTE V8 1955-1962 WORKSHOP MANUAL
FIAT 500 FACTORY WORKSHOP MANUAL 1957-1973
FIAT 600, 600D & MULTIPLA FACTORY WORKSHOP MANUAL 1955-1969
JAGUAR E-TYPE 3.8 & 4.2 SERIES 1 & 2 WORKSHOP MANUAL
JAGUAR MK 7, 8, 9 & XK120, 140, 150 WORKSHOP MANUAL 1948-1961
METROPOLITAN FACTORY WORKSHOP MANUAL
MGA & MGB OWNERS HANDBOOK & WORKSHOP MANUAL
MG MIDGET TC, TD, TF & TF1500 WORKSHOP MANUAL
PORSCHE 356 1948-1965 WORKSHOP MANUAL
PORSCHE 912 WORKSHOP MANUAL
TRIUMPH TR2, TR3, TR4 1953-1965 WORKSHOP MANUAL
VOLKSWAGEN TRANSPORTER, TRUCKS & WAGONS 1950-1979 WSM
VOLVO 1944-1968 ALL MODELS WORKSHOP MANUAL

VELOCEPRESS TECHNICAL BOOKS - AUTOMOBILE

FERRARI 250/GT SERVICE AND MAINTENANCE
FERRARI GUIDE TO PERFORMANCE
FERRARI OWNER'S HANDBOOK
FERRARI TUNING TIPS & MAINTENANCE TECHNIQUES
HOW TO BUILD A FIBERGLASS CAR
HOW TO BUILD A RACING CAR
HOW TO RESTORE THE MODEL 'A' FORD
MASERATI OWNER'S HANDBOOK
OBERT'S FIAT GUIDE
PERFORMANCE TUNING THE SUNBEAM TIGER
SOUPING THE VOLKSWAGEN
SOLEX CARBURETORS (EMPHASIS ON UK & EU AUTOMOBILES)
SU CARBURETORS (EMPHASIS ON UK AUTOMOBILES)
WEBER CARBURETORS (EMPHASIS ON ALFA & FIAT)

VELOCEPRESS BOOKS & GUIDES - AUTOMOBILE

ABARTH BUYERS GUIDE
COMPLETE CATALOG OF JAPANESE MOTOR VEHICLES
FERRARI 308 SERIES BUYER'S AND OWNER'S GUIDE
FERRARI BERLINETTA LUSSO
FERRARI BROCHURES AND SALES LITERATURE 1946-1967
FERRARI BROCHURES AND SALES LITERATURE 1968-1989
FERRARI OPP, MAINTENANCE & SERVICE H/BOOKS 1948-1963
FERRARI SERIAL NUMBERS PART I - ODD NUMBERS TO 21399
FERRARI SERIAL NUMBERS PART II - EVEN NUMBERS TO 1050
FERRARI SPYDER CALIFORNIA
HENRY'S FABULOUS MODEL "A" FORD
MASERATI BROCHURES AND SALES LITERATURE

VELOCEPRESS BOOKS – RACING

CARRERA PANAMERICANA - MEXICAN ROAD RACE (BOOK OF)
DIALED IN - THE JAN OPPERMAN STORY
IF HEMINGWAY HAD WRITTEN A RACING NOVEL
LE MANS 24 (THE BOOK THAT THE FILM WAS BASED ON)
VEDA ORR'S NEW REVISED HOT ROD PICTORIAL

AUTOBOOKS WORKSHOP MANUALS & BROOKLANDS ROAD TEST PORTFOLIOS

FOR A COMPLETE LISTING OF THE AUTOBOOKS & BROOKLANDS TITLES
THAT WE CURRENTLY HAVE AVAILABLE, PLEASE VISIT OUR WEBSITE.

For complete details of any of the titles listed above please visit our website at:
www.VelocePress.com

90,000 owners can't be wrong!

Cyclemaster was first marketed at the end of 1950. Since then an average of 600 sales have been made every week in Great Britain alone —and the demand is steadily being maintained. Cyclemaster, the **original engine-in-a-wheel**, has proved itself beyond doubt—to the public and to the trade. It is, indeed, the "Magic Wheel."

What is the secret of this success? No secret at all, really. Just the unbeatable formula of a first-class product backed by a Dealer organization 1,400 strong.

★ ★ ★

Cyclemaster can be fitted to any make of bicycle or tandem but additional manufacturing arrangements have been made with Mercury Industries Ltd. for two special bicycle models.

PILLION model for business use and weekend pleasure trips.

ROUNDSMAN—a special strong delivery bicycle for tradesmen. Taking payloads of up to 1 cwt., it offers speedy delivery at lowest possible operating costs.

★ ★ ★

Coloured leaflets of all models (giving full specification and prices) and a specimen copy of the Cyclemaster magazine, "The Magic Wheel" will be sent on request.

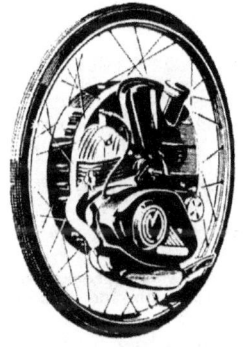

Cyclemaster

THE MAGIC WHEEL THAT WINGS YOUR HEEL

CYCLEMASTER LIMITED (Dept.: B.C.)
38a St. George's Drive, Victoria, London, S.W.1

THE *Britax Cycle*

Specially designed to take the DUCATI 'CUCCIOLO' CYCLE MOTOR

Fitted to an ordinary bicycle, the famous DUCATI "CUCCIOLO" CYCLE MOTOR will provide efficient and economical motive power beyond compare. Used in conjunction with the BRITAX CYCLE—specially *designed* for the job—The Ducati Cucciolo is "given its head"; for comfort, stability, *proved* reliability and maximum service, the combination of these two outstanding units fulfils every demand of the enthusiastic cycle motorist.

DUCATI "CUCCIOLO" CYCLE MOTOR

- 48 c.c. Four-stroke O.H.V. Engine
- 2-speed Pre-selector Gear Box
- Bottom Bracket Mounting for Maximum Stability
- Direct Chain Drive
- Incorporating 6-volt Dynamo Lighting
- Independent Lubrication (no need to mix petrol with oil)
- 250 m.p.g.
- Petrol Tank Capacity of 1¼ gallons

BRITAX CYCLE

- 19 in. Reinforced Heavy-gauge Steel Tube Frame
- Pressed Steel Girder Forks with Rubber Suspension and Rebound Damper
- Internal Expanding Hub Brakes
- 26 in. × 1¾ in. Wheels, with Ball-race Journal Hubs
- Super Comfort Autocycle Saddle
- Rust-proofed and Enamelled Frame: all Bright Parts Heavily Chromium Plated
- Supplied Complete with Number Plates, Rear Reflector, Front and Rear Lamps, Horn, Carrier, Inflator, Tool Bag and Tools

BRITAX (London) LTD., 115-129 Carlton Vale, London, N.W.6
Telephone: MAIda Vale 9351 (7 lines)

For STURDINESS... POWER... ECONOMY... RELIABILITY...

it's CYCLAID all the way!

SPECIFICATION

Motor: Single cylinder, two-stroke. Piston displacement: 31 c.c. Compression ratio: 1 : 5·6. Cylinder: Aluminium with special cast iron liner. Cylinder head: Aluminium, detachable. Ignition: Wipac Series '90' Magneto with lighting coil. Carburettor: Amal. Total reduction ratio : 1 : 18·5. Power transmission : Belt drive by endless rubber reinforced V belt. Fuel tank: capacity about 3 pints. Fuel: 1 part oil to 25 parts petrol. Continuous output: 0·7 h.p. at 3,500 r.p.m. Maximum speed: 18–20 m.p.h. Fuel consumption: 250 m.p.g. (approx.). Weight of the total installation: 18/20 lb. (approx.), complete with tank and all accessories.

RETAIL PRICE £24 NO PURCHASE TAX

The CYCLAID power unit is British designed and built throughout to precision limits.

BRITISH SALMSON CYCLAID LTD.

SALES: 76 Victoria St., S.W.1.   TATe Gallery 9138/9.
WORKS: Larkhall, Lanarkshire.

www.ingramcontent.com/pod-product-compliance
Lightning Source LLC
Chambersburg PA
CBHW070557170426
43201CB00012B/1867